T0328648

Cambridge Elements ☰

Elements in Intercultural Communication
edited by
Will Baker
University of Southampton
Troy McConachy
University of Warwick
Sonia Morán Panero
University of Southampton

SHORT-TERM STUDENT EXCHANGES AND INTERCULTURAL LEARNING

Gareth Humphreys
Sojo University

CAMBRIDGE
UNIVERSITY PRESS

Shaftesbury Road, Cambridge CB2 8EA, United Kingdom

One Liberty Plaza, 20th Floor, New York, NY 10006, USA

477 Williamstown Road, Port Melbourne, VIC 3207, Australia

314–321, 3rd Floor, Plot 3, Splendor Forum, Jasola District Centre, New Delhi – 110025, India

103 Penang Road, #05–06/07, Visioncrest Commercial, Singapore 238467

Cambridge University Press is part of Cambridge University Press & Assessment, a department of the University of Cambridge.

We share the University's mission to contribute to society through the pursuit of education, learning and research at the highest international levels of excellence.

www.cambridge.org
Information on this title: www.cambridge.org/9781009462594

DOI: 10.1017/9781009356671

First published 2023

A catalogue record for this publication is available from the British Library

ISBN 978-1-009-46259-4 Hardback
ISBN 978-1-009-35665-7 Paperback
ISSN 2752-5589 (online)
ISSN 2752-5570 (print)

Short-Term Student Exchanges and Intercultural Learning

Elements in Intercultural Communication

DOI: 10.1017/9781009356671
First published online: November 2023

Gareth Humphreys
Sojo University
Author for correspondence: Gareth Humphreys, ghumphreys@m.sojo-u.ac.jp

Abstract: Short-term student exchanges can offer valuable opportunities for intercultural learning and engagement in intercultural communication using English (the language focus in this Element). However, research and educational practices often assume that the most effective intercultural learning occurs through interactions with local individuals in 'target' culture learning and adherence to standard English language norms. These assumptions overlook important learning opportunities from interactions in culturally and linguistically diverse settings as features of many international exchange experiences. This Element proposes a perspective in student exchange research and practice that reflects this diversity and encompasses the intercultural learning model of intercultural awareness, intercultural citizenship education, and Global Englishes.

Keywords: student exchange, intercultural learning, higher education internationalisation, Global Englishes, study abroad

ISBNs: 9781009462594 (HB), 9781009356657 (PB), 9781009356671 (OC)
ISSNs: 2752-5589 (online), 2752-5570 (print)

Contents

1 Introduction and Conceptual Orientation

1.1 Introduction

Intercultural contact among individuals in multicultural and multilingual settings has increased as a consequence of new communication technology, travel opportunities, international business, student mobility, and other movement of people across national borders. As a result, many people today are regularly involved in online and offline, local and non-local, formal and informal intercultural communication with people from different cultural and linguistic backgrounds. This reality is recognised by many higher education (HE) institutions in processes of educational internationalisation that emphasise the need for effective communication in such contexts. These processes are regularly understood as the integration of an 'international, intercultural or global dimension into the purpose, functions or delivery of HE at the institutional and national levels' (Knight, 2008, p. 21). In practice, these dimensions are operationalised in highly varied ways at both national educational and institutional policy levels (Killick, 2015). One popular way in which universities address internationalisation is through the promotion of short-term student exchanges (i.e., temporary overseas educational sojourns for language study, research study, or cultural and study tours; contextualised in Section 2.3). These programmes can be varied in character, location, duration, programme add-ons, and learning objectives, and there is also wide variation in individual student experiences of exchange programmes.

These international experiences tend to be promoted by institutions and selected by students based on expectations of opportunities to engage in intercultural communication and learn from others. However, there are perspectives in education that simply sending students abroad is enough to support intercultural learning, overlooking the fact that being present in another country does not guarantee such learning will occur (e.g., Jones, 2017). Also problematic in exchange practices are perspectives that intercultural learning is more effective following interactions with local (native speaker) individuals, despite how in many experiences the potential learning through interactions with other international students in multicultural settings is more significant (see Section 1.2.2). In intercultural learning following student interactions with others during exchanges, language (commonly English, the language focus in this Element) plays a key role. In these interactions, English language use tends to be characterised by variability rather than adherence to standard norms, as promoted in conventional educational practices (see Section 1.2.3) (e.g., Rose & Galloway, 2019). In addition, English may be used alongside other languages in multilingual communication during student exchanges. The variability in

English use and the cultural diversity among English users highlight that there is no fixed target culture or standard way of using English. As such, educational focus on fact-based culture learning and standard language use contradicts the communication realities of English use in a multicultural world and is unlikely to equip students for effective engagement in intercultural communication in diverse contexts. Such target-based learning is also unlikely to result in any connection with intercultural citizenship (i.e., a sense of citizenship beyond national borders and empathy with, and responsibility towards, other individuals and communities in the world). Intercultural citizenship is a significant goal of international education (e.g., Killick, 2015), and can be found among HE internationalisation policies throughout the world. Thus, there is a need for this to be reflected in educational practices, particularly in connection with student exchanges.

In this Element, I (the author, and a British teacher–researcher in Japan) argue that target learning focus on national cultures and standard ways of using English overlook cultural and linguistic diversity associated with English language use and its users. I explore how student exchanges can lead to intercultural learning and changes in perspectives towards using English in communication. This exploration is potentially important to encourage exchange research and practices to embrace the diversity in English use and users globally and recognise multicultural and multilingual aspects of student exchange experiences.

1.2 Key Conceptual Areas

To develop these points, I first offer a basic characterisation of key terms as they are understood here as context for a more in-depth discussion, which follows.

1.2.1 Culture, Intercultural Communication, and Identity

In educational contexts, 'culture' is frequently regarded as the collective knowledge, traits, and characteristics that individuals inherently possess due to their association with specific (national) groups. In such educational treatment, emphasis on national cultural differences risks cultural essentialism; that is, 'presuming that there is a universal essence, homogeneity, and unity in a particular culture' (Holliday, Hyde & Kullman, 2021, p. 1). This treatment of culture connects less with developing skills to interact in a multicultural world and more with stereotyping; i.e., 'overgeneralizations of group characteristics or behaviors, which are applied to individuals of those groups' (Hughes & Baldwin, 2002, p. 114). Moreover, it overlooks differences among individuals from particular settings as well as differences in how meaning is contested among individuals. These concerns are also relevant to intercultural and related cross-cultural research, where over the last seventy years, nation-based cultural understandings around 'facts' have been common in comparisons of 'distinct' cultures described at the level of nation; that is, descriptions of cultures on a national level based without acknowledging complexity and diversity within national cultures (Piller, 2017). While 'intercultural' and 'cross-cultural' are sometimes used synonymously, there are more tendencies in cross-cultural approaches to handle culture within fixed geographical lines, contrasting individuals in one community with those in another, and presupposing that such individuals will be inherently 'different'.

I argue that individual identities and their relationships with cultures are more complex than can be represented by fixed labelling. As such, throughout I use 'intercultural' based on an understanding that cultural differences do not necessarily represent problems and that any differences in communication are interaction-based. This position is informed by Zhu's (2019) view of intercultural communication as dynamic, emergent, and negotiated among individuals who are concurrently members of a range of categories (e.g., ethnicity, gender, religion, age, socioeconomic status, education level, and occupation, among others) that may or may not be relevant in particular moments of interaction. Identities are, therefore, complex, multifaceted, and go beyond national descriptions since individuals negotiate and navigate their identities in contexts of communication (Zhu, 2019). This perspective underscores the necessity for individuals to acknowledge a diversity of identities that emerge in intercultural communication.

1.2.2 Intercultural Learning

To avoid nation-based conceptions of cultures and languages and to represent them as fluid in intercultural communication, I refer to Baker's (2011) intercultural awareness (ICA) to conceptualise intercultural learning. This is defined as: 'a conscious understanding of the role culturally based forms, practices and frames of reference can have in intercultural communication, and an ability to put these conceptions into practice in a flexible and context specific manner in communication' (Baker, 2011, p. 202). Thus, ICA recognises intercultural communication as driven by the functional needs of those involved, irrespective of cultural or linguistic background and it emphasises flexibility in relation to emergent communicative practices. Importantly, it does not provide specific details of how 'forms', 'practices', and 'frames of reference' should be understood in terms of 'competence', given controversies in how 'competence' is constituted (see discussion in Section 2.4; Baker, 2015). This flexibility can be crucial in exchange contexts that are marked by cultural and linguistic diversity, where complex interactions go beyond static and pre-learnt fact-based categories of knowledge and fixed ways of using English in communication. A detailed overview of ICA is provided in Section 2.6.

I also explore how student exchanges can influence connections with other individuals and communities; that is, global/intercultural citizenship (used interchangeably, though I use intercultural citizenship for its links to the discussion on intercultural citizenship education (Byram, 2008 in Section 3.4). Intercultural citizenship education is based on preparing individuals to navigate an increasingly diverse and interconnected world by supporting the development of skills to understand and engage with individuals in multicultural contexts, and to become active, responsible citizens in multicultural communities. Its prominence in the internationalisation aims of many universities means it is a key area for exploration in student exchange research, though currently somewhat underrepresented.

1.2.3 ELF/EMF and Global Englishes

Despite the essential role of language in facilitating intercultural learning during interactions with others, its role in research on intercultural learning is frequently disregarded (Baker & Ishikawa, 2021). To address this here, I focus on an integration of intercultural learning and intercultural communication using English based on contemporary perspectives towards English use in global contexts (e.g., Jenkins, 2015a; Rose & Galloway, 2019). Exchanges offer opportunities for students to form new perspectives towards English use in line with Global Englishes (GE), defined as 'the linguistic and sociocultural dimensions of global uses, usages and users of English' (University of Southampton, 2023). In accordance with GE, I adopt the view that English use is not standardised and singular, but variability and multilingualism are the reality for communication involving English in most global contexts (e.g., Baker & Ishikawa, 2021). These aspects of English use are reflected in research on English as a lingua franca (ELF) and English as a multi-lingua franca (EMF) communication; that is, 'multilingual communication in which English is available as a contact language of choice, but is not necessarily chosen' (Jenkins, 2015a, p. 73; see Section 3.2). While some exchange students may engage with local English native[1] speakers and focus on 'standard' language use, on other programmes, students find themselves studying alongside and

---

[1] I acknowledge that there are complex distinctions between 'native' and 'non-native' English users, particularly in relation to language ownership, legitimacy of language practices, and ELF/ EMF.

socialising with other international students and using ELF/EMF in communication. In this way, communication practices contrast with prescriptivist standard language use that continues to characterise English language teaching (ELT) and learning (Rose & Galloway, 2019). Awareness and understanding of GE themes and practices, then, encompass pluralistic over monolithic understandings of English, recognition and acceptance of diversity and variability in English language use, and use of ELF/EMF in communication. These issues are discussed in detail in Sections 3.2 and 3.3.

1.3 Positionality

The critical perspective that I adopt towards student exchange practices, culture in education, and ELT necessitates reflection on my own positionality as a teacher–researcher in Japan and as author of this Element. This involves identifying and questioning my own background, preconceptions, and biases and acknowledging their influence on this Element. However, this is not a 'stable' or 'once-for-all process' (Babaii, 2018, p. 46), and readers will, inevitably, consider who I am in ways that are different to how I think about myself as I write this. Firstly, my nationality is British, though for about twenty years I have mostly lived outside the United Kingdom, firstly as a student, then as a teacher, and later as a teacher–researcher, in Mexico, Bolivia, Spain, Angola, Vietnam, and now Japan. Most of my formal education was UK-based. I am also a native English speaker. I am aware that this background and status have been advantageous in hiring decisions (see also Yazan & Rudolph, 2018) and that my employment may be seen to reinforce inequalities around notions of ideal English language teachers (Selvi, 2010). Central to this inequality is the perception that I use English 'correctly' and that I represent a native-English-speaking (national) culture, but the concept of 'correct' English and this educational representation of a singular national culture fail to recognise fluidity and diversity of English use in global contexts.

In the beginning of my teaching career, my teaching practices centred on the promotion of standard norms of English use according to particular assessment frameworks utilised institutionally, and this included 'penalising' language 'errors'. As I gained more teaching experience and engaged in further study and professional reflection, I developed awareness of GE. This awareness is now reflected, within the constraints of curriculum and assessment frameworks, in my classroom practices, including accepting and not 'correcting' individual language practices. Recently, my role within a language learning centre has changed, and I have been involved in designing intercultural educational options. While this role may have been better suited to a local educator, there are professional expectations within the setting that require me to be involved in such curricular development. I acknowledge, however, that my involvement is influenced by elements of my cultural, educational, and professional background. This influence may be perceived as educationally colonialist in that I might 'impose' particular perspectives on students, even if my teaching and research practices are 'well-intentioned' (e.g., Gorski, 2008). Nonetheless, as a cultural 'outsider' it is also my view that I can offer perspectives and experiences of potential interest and relevance to students in my educational setting. Indeed, my professional role at a Japanese university is based on expectations that I will contribute to an international campus by presenting myself in 'international' ways (i.e., I will look 'Western', speak English, and I will act 'differently'). The tension between these realities and my particular conceptual awareness arises from the potential for my actions and perspectives to reinforce unequal power relations. As such, I must manage my complex role while constantly self-reflecting and critically engaging with the local context and the experiences and perspectives of my students.

There is a clear need for research from diverse local perspectives in different educational settings regarding internationalisation, intercultural learning, and language education, and these perspectives can offer alternative and valuable insights about the world (Risager, 2022). However, there is also an impact of international mobility on research since investigations on particular regions are not always conducted by researchers based in or from that region, or limited to researchers who are physically present in particular regions, or who share the same cultural background as those being studied (Rose, Sahan & Zhou, 2022). While research from diverse perspectives is important, as a teacher–researcher (with teaching being my central professional role) from the United Kingdom and working in Japan, my perspectives on the 'front line' of language and intercultural education can potentially connect with other individuals who are reflecting on their own educational practices or practices within their institutions. Readers should, however, consider this positionality section as they draw their own conclusions about how this work may have application elsewhere. Readers should also note that it is not my intention to urge all others to work within the frameworks I discuss, nor do I consider other approaches inherently 'wrong'. I may be critical of certain practices, but I also recognise meaning and value in research that differs from my own conceptual position.

1.4 Element Aim and Outline

In this Element, I discuss student exchange experiences linked to ICA, intercultural citizenship, and GE (particularly ELF/EMF). I offer theoretical but empirically grounded arguments as to why these areas are important for learning on student exchanges. My central arguments are: (1) short-term international exchange experiences in culturally and linguistically diverse contexts offer more meaningful learning experiences (in terms of how they are perceived by students) than target culture/language educational approaches; (2) essentialist approaches to culture and language learning (in institutional and exchange-based practices) overlook the multilingual and multicultural character of many developmental experiences on student exchange; and (3), systematically designed intercultural education based on ICA, intercultural citizenship education, and GE is highly relevant to support exchange learning.

Following this introduction, the Element is divided into four more sections. In Section 2, I explore student exchanges and intercultural learning in the context of HE internationalisation in Section 2.2. In Section 2.3, I offer a characterisation of particular exchange types and practices before exploring multicultural and multilingual realities of many exchange experiences in Section 2.4. In Section 2.5, I look at intercultural learning and exchange research and then provide more detail on ICA in Section 2.6. In Section 3, I discuss intercultural and GE education, which, for context, first involves focus on multilingual communication and the role of ELF/EMF (Section 3.2). I contrast conventional educational approaches with particular contemporary pedagogical frameworks related to my conceptual position in Section 3.3. In Section 3.4, I relate these approaches to student exchange learning, and highlight intercultural citizenship education as important in the context of student exchange learning. In Section 4, I present a case study from Japan, situated in HE internationalisation policies and local educational practices. I draw on ICA, intercultural citizenship, and GE in an analysis of the experiences of fifteen students participating in student exchange programmes. This analysis also involves exploration of the conditions for learning in these areas in student reports of experiences before, during, and after their sojourns (i.e., trajectories through student exchanges). Thus, there is a focus on both individual learning and institutional practices. In Section 5, I present some recommendations for both research and practice based on the findings from the case study, and I outline some specific learning activities that may be useful to other practitioners in supporting exchange students.

2 Intercultural Learning on Short-Term Student Exchanges

2.1 Introduction

Having outlined the conceptual orientation, I now provide a contextualisation of student exchange practices and related terms. Thereafter, I discuss multicultural and multilingual aspects of exchange experiences. I then focus on different approaches to intercultural learning, including ICA.

2.2 Higher Education Internationalisation

In Section 1.1, Knight (2008) offered a widely cited definition of HE internationalisation based on integrating international, intercultural, or global dimensions into the purpose, function, and delivery of HE. Based on this definition, I understand the global dimension as representing a flow of knowledge and technology between countries, market integration, and the movement of people across borders for work or other purposes (Rodrik, 2011). In contrast, the international dimension concerns foreign language education, increasing diversity among students and teachers on campuses (e.g., Ferguson, 2007), and links to student mobility; that is, students crossing national borders for educational purposes (Kelo, Teichler & Wächter, 2006). These international aspects are sometimes criticised as primarily motivated by financial benefits or on presenting the image of an international profile, particularly via quantitative increases of international staff and students on campuses (Ferguson, 2007). Furthermore, there are perceptions in some contexts that hiring international staff can be 'tokenistic' and 'symbolic', to appear on the surface to meet internationalisation claims (Brotherhood, Hammond & Kim, 2019, p. 507). However, these increases may not be accompanied by internationalisation initiatives led by international staff, particularly in settings where integration of international staff within institutions is limited (Mihut, de Gayardon & Rudt, 2017).

The intercultural aspects tend to be more educationally focused than other aspects of internationalisation and include curricular initiatives. There can be considerable variation in how these are operationalised due to obstacles and opportunities that can exist within geographical or institutional contexts. Potential obstacles include a lack of resources, especially if initiatives require significant financial and personnel resources. The effectiveness of any initiative is also influenced by the quality of training for teachers, particularly when training is based on outmoded views of intercultural learning (Alismail, 2016). Opportunities to support the intercultural dimension include research-informed and locally relevant training for staff, curricular integration of intercultural learning to provide opportunities for students to engage with diverse perspectives, and intercultural educational collaborations with institutions in other settings to facilitate intercultural exchange; that is, initiatives where students from different backgrounds engage with one another, sharing their experiences and perspectives. During student exchanges, opportunities and challenges can relate to types of social contact available, educational systems around exchanges, and social and educational support while overseas.

These dimensions can commonly be found in university website statements on internationalisation throughout the world. However, these statements may also be used for institutional marketing purposes in the use of 'attractive' terms for prospective students around globally engaged graduates with skills to work in multicultural settings (Dippold et al., 2019, p. 314). Following a brief internet search of three randomly selected universities from twelve different countries, I identified the intercultural dimension among internationalisation statements in Table 1 (accurate at the time of writing; some statements translated).

The range of settings in Table 1 clarifies the wide variation in these HE policies, both between and within nations. Some statements explicitly link to national citizenship and local responsibilities, while others focus on academic relationships with other universities. Nonetheless, many of these statements connect with developing responsibilities to communities beyond national borders (i.e., intercultural citizenship). Most statements in Table 1 do not specifically mention language learning, but at many institutions the achievement of these policies is in part linked to language learning. Given the global spread of English, for many students the language learning focus is English.

2.3 Short-Term Student Exchanges

Student mobility is a critical area of internationalisation in HE, encompassing a range of activities such as study abroad programmes; that is, 'temporary sojourn[s] of pre-defined duration, undertaken for educational purposes' (Kinginger, 2009, p. 11). In associated research and practice, there can be a lack of delineation between programme types where 'study abroad' is used unproblematically as an 'umbrella' term for all programme types even when it is not apparent what study, if any, has taken place (Engle & Engle, 2003, p. 3). This situation is reflected in certain institutional practices where the lack of borderlines between distinct programme types can result in a lack of clarity among students regarding programme distinctions. Consequently, students may not understand the limitations of their programme and may have unrealistic expectations, particularly about the amount of contact, and type of contact, they will experience with others. 'Student exchange', as a related term, is sometimes used for reciprocal agreements between universities for students to study for a period at a partner university. Some practitioners also consider it to be an inaccurate synonym for study abroad (Forum on Education Abroad, 2011). Despite these perspectives, I use 'short-term student exchange' (elsewhere 'student exchange' or 'exchange') to represent short overseas programmes of

Table 1 Intercultural dimension in institutional website statements

Brazil	i.	Innovation and the development of global competences; planning their global career and the advantages of being a citizen of the world (Anhembi Morumbi University).
	ii.	Contribute to national and international solidarity (Federal University of Rio de Janeiro).
	iii.	Respect for difference; social responsibility; building futures based on a dialogue with the present, in the local and global spheres (Federal University of Rio Grande do Sul).
China	i.	Promote international collaboration and engagement (Central South University).
	ii.	Nurture global-minded responsible people who are strong in cross-cultural communication (Guangdong University of Foreign Studies).
	iii.	Cultivating global citizens who will thrive in today's world (Tsinghua University).
Colombia	i.	The promotion of solidarity, inclusion; the formation of citizens with a global sense (CES University).
	ii.	Act responsibly in the face of the requirements and trends of the contemporary world, and creatively lead processes of change (National University of Colombia).
	iii.	Promote knowledge, creation, and reaffirmation of regional, national and universal values (University of Tolima).
Egypt	i.	Supporting academic freedom in the context of social responsibility and respect for others; fostering a culture of tolerance (Alexandria University).
	ii.	Achieving excellence and leadership locally and internationally for producing a knowledgeable society, effective community partnerships and internationalisation (Mansoura University).
	iii.	Fairness and civility towards others while recognising and embracing each individual's dignity, freedom, and diversity; expose students to the real world and its diversity (Misr University for Science & Technology).
Germany	i.	Intercultural openness, equal opportunities, and mutual respect; respectful communication (Bielefeld University).
	ii.	We see ourselves as Europeans and global citizens (University of Freiburg).
	iii.	Remain rooted in the community while becoming agents of change in the world; opportunity for intercultural learning and language ability (Humboldt University of Berlin).

Table 1 (cont.)

India	i.	Serve humanity through the creation of well-rounded, multi-skilled and socially responsible global citizens; sustained engagement with local, national, and global communities (University of Delhi).
	ii.	Contribute effectively to the welfare of society, address the local and global challenges; respecting culture (University of Mumbai).
	iii.	Creation of infrastructure for global competence (University of Rajasthan).
Japan	i.	Enhance integrated education of global-minded human resources; aim to increase students' global competency to prepare graduates to play an active role in the international arena (Hiroshima University).
	ii.	Cultivating individuals equipped with international mindsets and making contributions to solve both domestic and global challenges (Keio University).
	iii.	Foster individuals capable of exercising leadership both in the domestic and international arenas so they can contribute to human welfare (Nagoya University).
Mexico	i.	Social responsibility, transparency, and accountability in the locality, the region, the country, and the world (Autonomous University of San Luis Potosí).
	ii.	Cultural cooperation with national and foreign individuals, institutions, and organisations, based on reciprocity (University of Colima).
	iii.	Civic formation of students, extending their participation in both the local and the global scene (University of Guadalajara).
South Africa	i.	Development of graduates who are aware of the wider world and who have a sense of responsibility and commitment to making constructive contributions at the local, national, continental, and global level (Rhodes University).
	ii.	The development of a global citizenry (Stellenbosch University).
	iii.	Promote students' awareness of themselves as future citizens of the world with a motivation to work for social justice (University of Cape Town).
Thailand	i.	Responsibility to society at local and national and international levels (Chulalongkorn University).

Table 1 (cont.)

	ii.	Produce graduates who are good citizens of the global society (King Mongkut's University of Technology).
	iii.	Empower and prepare students for international environments; emphasise diverse work integration; preserve individual nationalities with recognition of their cultural differences (Siam University).
UK	i.	Enable our students to become 'global citizens' (Cardiff University).
	ii.	Commitment to global connectedness and collaboration (University of Glasgow).
	iii.	Think and act both locally and across borders and cultures to promote the development of a global mindset (University of Nottingham).
US	i.	Encourage our students to be global (University of Hawai'i).
	ii.	Enhance core competencies that will distinguish them as global citizens including global knowledge, global engagement, and global responsibility (University of Houston).
	iii.	Global engagement to enact positive change in our communities locally, nationally, and internationally (University of Washington).

a few days to up to one month. I prefer this term over variations due to the specific emphasis on the short duration of programmes and because these programmes do not always have a clear focus on study. In practice, some programmes may only be a few days long, but they are often considered short-term student exchange programmes (institutionally and in research) if they involve travel to another country. This interest in short-term programmes is supported by a trend towards participation in shorter overseas programmes and a decrease in the proportion of long-term participation in overall numbers (Perry, Stoner & Tarrant, 2012). In addition, some students can only participate in very brief programmes based on, for example, other commitments or financial constraints, but may still have opportunities to gain valuable experiences and insights that contribute to intercultural learning. Finally, I believe this focus is important in terms of building understandings of short-term programmes, particularly as long-term and short-term (as well as micro-term) programmes often share similar objectives of providing access to, and connections with, learning opportunities in international settings (Slotkin, Durie & Eisenberg, 2012).

The student exchange focus here includes intensive language learning courses at universities and commercial language academies, educational or cultural tours involving lessons with local teachers and informal activities organised with students in host settings, research-based trips where participants attend classes at selected institutions, and field trips. The language focus on the programmes discussed in this Element is English, but destinations are not limited to locations where English is widely used as a first language. Participants may also study alongside English users from other countries, or they may study in intact faculty-led groups in tailored courses with classmates from their home universities. The extent to which student exchanges lead to intercultural learning or provide opportunities to use English in intercultural communication is likely to vary based on contextual factors on exchange programmes (as well as on differences among individuals participating; e.g., Koyanagi, 2018). On some programmes, there are few opportunities to connect with others. For example, tailored courses with classmates from home universities can be 'inherently limiting' if there are few interactions with individuals from outside the group (Cubillos & Ilvento, 2018, p. 260). These approaches may, therefore, prevent engagement with new perspectives (Isabelli-García, 2006). There may also be a holiday mentality to sojourns (Day, 1987), with a focus on visiting new places rather than on opportunities for new learning through interaction (Engle & Engle, 2003). Where intercultural communication does occur on these kinds of programmes, it is often in organised, brief, cultural exchange events where communication can be superficial (Allen, 2010). These kinds of events, which may include attending a traditional dance performance or trying local cuisine, may help students learn about aspects of local cultures, but they are unlikely to facilitate deeper intercultural understanding and may, I argue, perpetuate stereotypes.

More extensive intercultural communication is likely to be available on language study or research-based programmes where students participate in programmes managed by host settings, and where students travel independently or in small groups rather than in large groups on programmes organised and led by the home university. There may also be homestay arrangements, which as Kinginger (2009) states, are often perceived as an advantage for communication opportunities (though there can also be complaints about spending time alone in such settings). It should also be noted that participation in international study programmes (of whichever type) does not guarantee intercultural learning will occur (Jackson, 2020; Jones, 2017). Students may have negative intercultural experiences abroad and withdraw from seeking further communication opportunities, or they may be inclined to maintain significant contact with home using communication technology (Kinginger, 2009). On programmes themselves, intercultural learning may not be a priority on exchange experiences outsourced to commercial providers, with a more touristic and profit-based than educational focus (Pipitone, 2018).

Additionally, not all students have access to exchange opportunities, including the necessary financial resources (though funding options may be available for students in some settings) (Lörz, Netz & Quast, 2016). Indeed, there are likely to be many students throughout the world who want to develop international connections through international exchange, but whose circumstances prevent them from doing so. As an important side point, these issues highlight the need for intercultural learning options to be provided in home-based curricula for all students, not only those who are able to participate in overseas study (e.g., De Wit, 2020). These 'internationalisation-at-home' initiatives are defined by Beelen and Jones (2015) as the 'integration of international/intercultural dimensions into the formal/informal curriculum for all students within domestic learning environments' (p. 69). In practice, initiatives can involve local and international students collaborating on coursework tasks or co-curricular activities (Soria & Troisi, 2014). Digital educational options provide other opportunities, for example, in virtual exchanges, also referred to as collaborative online international learning, online intercultural exchange, or telecollaboration. In associated educational initiatives, students engage in tasks (e.g., discussions, intercultural exchanges) with individuals in other geographical locations, connecting via email, social media, or online forums. The use of digital resources within HE is often perceived to enhance learning experiences (e.g., Mondi, Woods & Rafi, 2007), which, coupled with the wide student use of personal devices in many settings, means it often makes sense to offer opportunities for online engagement with intercultural content in home university-based learning.

2.4 Multicultural and Multilingual Realities of Student Exchange

Also problematic in exchange-related research and practice are assumptions that learning should be focused on interactions with local 'target' native speakers and 'target' members of host (national) cultures. Indeed, contact with native language users from destination communities is often considered the ideal way to support development (e.g., Donnelly-Smith, 2009); that is, when students 'really 'experience' the host culture by truly engaging with host country participants' (Heinzmann, Künzle, Schallhart & Müller, 2015, p. 188). In terms of language learning, standard and fixed language practices continue to provide the basis for exchange-related learning in many settings (Trentman & Diao, 2021). These assumptions about both target culture and language learning can be found in statements on exchange programme websites highlighting immersion in local cultures, connections with local individuals, and learning from native speakers. They include the following extracts from selected exchange websites focusing on English-language learning and associated with the case study in Section 4 (accessed via documentation in the university's international centre; institutional names removed):

- To be effective at learning a language, you should be totally immersed in the local culture (UK language programme).
- Communicating with locals in their native language helps to build relationships and gain a deeper understanding of their culture (US language programme).
- If you choose to study English abroad, you'll be surrounded 24/7 by native speakers, in a new, exciting culture (US language programme).
- Learning a language from a native speaker allows you to pick up on nuances and colloquialisms that are difficult to learn from textbooks (US language programme).
- You will learn the language authentically when you talk to native speakers (US language programme).
- Immersing yourself in a language environment with native speakers is the most effective way to learn a new language (Australia language programme).
- Learning from a native speaker can fast track a student's language ability (Australia language programme).
- The fastest way to learn English is to surround yourself with native speakers (Canada language programme).
- Real-life immersion requires students to improve their skills to be understood by locals (UK language programme).
- While studying abroad, students communicate daily with locals and their colloquial, mumbled, or insanely fast (read, real) accents (US language programme).

These statements reflect the objectives of many exchange students to form connections with, and learn from, local native speaker individuals in host settings (e.g., Mitchell, McManus & Tracy-Ventura, 2015). Problematically, these objectives can be based on unquestioned beliefs that interactions with native speakers lead to more effective learning, and that these interactions should be the goal of participating in an exchange.[2] These beliefs are widely held and now 'embedded in ideas and practices' around student mobility

---

[2] There may be perceptions that student objectives to develop native-like proficiency are legitimate and that my perspective towards English learning is limiting. I argue, however, that there are diverse motivations and goals of English language learners, and there is a need to embrace a respectful approach that recognises the legitimacy of a wide range of ways English is used, and which recognises ELF/EMF.

(Kubota, 2016, p. 348). However, many exchange experiences involve merely brief or superficial contact with native speakers (Baker-Smemoe et al., 2014), and many participants do not have 'immersive' experiences due to challenges connecting with these language users, only using the language within classrooms (Kuntz & Belnap, 2001). In such scenarios, students who aim to connect with, and learn from, native language users but who are unable to do so may consider it a failure of their experience (Çiftçi & Karaman, 2018).

Despite these views, it has been found that intensive language learning can be supported without interactions with local native speakers (Llanes, Arnó & Mancho-Barés, 2016). Indeed, for many students, the main inter-locutors during student exchanges are other non-native language users (e.g., Kubota, 2016), and these interactions can represent important learning opportunities. Such connections tend to be based on more socialisation opportunities (Schartner, 2016), though students may also be more drawn to other students than local individuals (Csizer & Kontra, 2012), particularly if communication is perceived as more balanced; that is, that language 'errors' are considered more acceptable than in communication with native language users (Humphreys, 2022). Moreover, the use of ELF/EMF on these kinds of short programmes has been highlighted as common (Mocanu & Llurda, 2020). Thus, connections between 'target' culture and 'target' language use are challenged by the multicultural and multilingual character of exchange experiences and the varied interactions that can be available. These interactions are likely to lead to learning beyond target-culture learning or language development in association with local native speakers. In the context of global English use, individual multilingual resources are used in varied and unpredictable intercultural communication, beyond 'target' bounded cultural practices and standard language use commonly represented in ELT. These aspects of a sojourn can be highly meaningful for intercultural learning.

2.5 Student Exchange Research and Intercultural Learning

Research on intercultural learning and student exchanges emerged from research focused on the connections between study-abroad contexts and language learning, typically using pre- and post-tests to examine language gains (Carroll, 1967). Similar methodologies are applied to large-scale intercultural or cross-cultural research in which researchers select from developmental models representing distinct approaches to learning and development. However, the range of models to select from can be overwhelming for researchers, including those in the following 'partial list' (Dorsett, Larmar & Clark, 2019; Fantini, 2012):

- anxiety/uncertainty management model
- cross-cultural adaptation
- cross-cultural awareness
- cross-cultural competence
- cross-cultural knowledge
- cross-cultural sensitivity
- cultural awareness
- cultural competence
- cultural humility
- cultural intelligence
- cultural or intercultural sensitivity
- cultural safety
- cultural sensitivity
- effective intergroup communication
- ethnorelativity
- global awareness
- global competence
- global competitive intelligence
- global mindedness
- intercultural communicative competence
- intercultural cooperation
- intercultural development inventory
- intercultural effectiveness
- intercultural interaction
- intercultural practice
- intercultural sensitivity
- metaphoric competence
- multicultural competence
- pyramid model of intercultural competence

Research applying particular models to exchange experiences has led to varied outcomes, including findings that longer sojourns lead to more global mindedness (i.e., the skills to interact effectively in global environments; Kehl & Morris, 2008). While the duration of the programme can be a factor for intercultural learning, i.e., longer programmes lead to more intercultural learning opportunities, shorter sojourns have been seen to impact on cross-cultural sensitivity among participants (Anderson et al., 2006). In other studies of short-term programmes, a qualitatively analysed survey of 827 students showed developments in global awareness (Chieffo & Griffith, 2004). Similarly, cross-cultural knowledge and competence developed from short programmes among 607 students in programmes of three to four weeks (Kurt, Olitsky & Geis, 2013). Developments were also reported among 136 students using pre- and post-tests in global awareness and cultural awareness following international study experiences (Gaia, 2015). Relatedly, in a longitudinal online questionnaire study among US-based undergraduate student teachers, self-assessed developments in cross-cultural awareness were reported following experiences abroad (Shiveley & Misco, 2015). In Japan, a mixed methods study involving twenty-nine Japanese students taking part in short-term programmes showed participants' beliefs that short-term overseas study experiences had expanded their worldviews (Koyanagi, 2018).

While these approaches broadly share objectives around developing tolerance and openness towards others, there can be ambiguity around terms used,
such as what constitutes 'development', 'learning', 'skill', and 'competence',
and how they should be defined in research. 'Development' is often related to
intercultural 'competence', but there are different conceptions of competence
and different understandings around how it is assessable in terms of development, or if indeed it should be assessed at all (Trede, Bowles & Bridges, 2013).
Controversies arise about the way that 'competence' and 'skill' are often treated
in fixed categories of analysis, while 'development' and 'learning' are used to
examine how students demonstrate these competences or skills. The 'measurement' of these areas relies on criteria that might not accurately capture the
complexity of individual intercultural learning, and different research perspectives can also influence what is considered 'competent' behavior. A number of
assessment models include standardised and quantifiable features so that survey
responses or some 'observable behaviour' in particular moments can be ana-
lysed/assessed. In this way, intercultural development is viewed as a linear
process through which an individual progresses through scales of 'competence'
by meeting specific criteria, implying development occurs in the same ways, in
the same order, for all people. This approach to development also implies some
'deficit' among 'baseline' students, in which deficit is identified by practitioners
(though not necessarily by students themselves; Jones, 2017). Standardised
assessment procedures can also contain biases in the original design based on
a particular research intent or conceptual perspective (Fantini, 2012). If the
same procedures are used without consideration of how different research
questions and contexts might be better suited to different methods, it is potentially problematic for research reliability. These approaches can also treat
exchange contexts as fixed, without accommodating particular variables of
relevance to individual learning (e.g., aspects of an individual's background,
prior experiences with intercultural communication, level of social support, and
access to resources).

A more flexible understanding of intercultural learning can recognise processes of learning and development beyond static measurements of competence. Moreover, flexible understandings in open research can prevent
a decontextualisation of important individual experiences by recognising the
subjectivity inherent in individually meaningful learning, rather than attempting
to measure intercultural learning objectively (Zotzmann, 2015). Conducting
research in ways that enable individual aspects and particular contextual variables (as they are reported by participants) to provide insight can then lead to
more in-depth outcomes (e.g., Coleman, 2013; Kinginger, 2009). In doing so,
students' own understandings of development can be insightful, instead of

defining development according to particular fixed and closed models. Jackson (2020) explains that more open and case-driven research can also accommodate individual differences in personality, motivation, previous intercultural experiences, identity, and background, while also accounting for contextual variables such as location, duration, programme type, accommodation situation, and social contact during exchanges. Thus, insight emerges from explorations of particular aspects and processes involved in exchange experiences rather than a focus on what can be 'measured' post-sojourn (Kinginger, 2009). This focus on the particularity of experiences may not allow for generalisability, though I believe this is a strength rather than a limitation of qualitative student exchange research.

2.6 Intercultural Awareness

In a non-target culture approach here, intercultural learning is conceptualised through Baker's (2011) model of ICA, which characterises knowledge, skills, and attitudes for intercultural communication (see Figure 1). It is not a static developmental model and learning is not treated in terms of fixed truths from a 'baseline' in a straight line towards some end point on a development model by meeting some form of 'competence' criteria. The ICA model provides an alternative approach that recognises the complexity, fluidity, and individual character of intercultural learning and communication. Despite its structure, its flexibility, adaptability, and broad categories ensure it does not fall into the traps of the more rigid approaches to intercultural development I have identified in Section 2.4. The model can thus be used in research that recognises complexity in individual experiences and learning.

According to Baker (2015), the twelve components across three levels build from a basic cultural awareness in level one (as per Figure 1), which is concerned with a general understanding of culture and how an individual's linguistic and cultural background can influence behaviour, beliefs, and values. Here, there could be awareness of differences among cultures (at the national level) and an ability to make general comparisons between one's own culture and 'others' (although this may be in generalisations or stereotypes). Level one does not include specific knowledge of other cultures, or about the concept of culture itself. Level two is based on an awareness of cultures as comprising diverse groups (beyond solely national groupings) in a more complex understanding of cultures and communication. Here, there is recognition of individuals as members of multiple groupings and also recognition of commonalities among people. At this level, individuals are aware of the fluid and relative nature of cultural understandings. Specific cultural knowledge can be utilised

---

Level One: Basic Cultural Awareness
An awareness of:
1 culture as a set of shared behaviours, beliefs, and values;
2 the role culture and context play in any interpretation of meaning;
3 our own culturally induced behaviour, values, and beliefs and the ability to articulate this;
4 others' culturally induced behaviour, values, and beliefs and the ability to compare this with our own culturally induced behaviour, values, and beliefs.

Level Two: Advanced Cultural Awareness
An awareness of:
5 the relative nature of cultural norms;
6 cultural understanding as provisional and open to revision;
7 multiple voices or perspectives within any cultural grouping;
8 individuals as members of many social groupings including cultural ones;
9 common ground between specific cultures as well as an awareness of possibilities for mismatch and miscommunication between specific cultures.

Level Three: Intercultural Awareness
An awareness of:
10 culturally based frames of reference, forms, and communicative practices as being related both to specific cultures and also as emergent and hybrid in intercultural communication;
11 initial interaction in intercultural communication as possibly based on cultural stereotypes or generalisations but an ability to move beyond these through;
12 a capacity to negotiate and mediate between different emergent socioculturally grounded communication modes and frames of reference based on the above understanding of culture in intercultural communication.

Figure 1 Twelve components of intercultural awareness according to Baker
(adapted from Baker, 2015, p. 164).

beyond generalisations to predict possible misunderstandings or miscommunications in specific instances of intercultural communication. The final level (level three) recognises that cultural references and communicative practices in intercultural communication may or may not be related to specific cultures. Here, individuals 'mediate and negotiate between different cultural frames of reference and communicative practices as they occur in specific examples of intercultural communication' (Baker, 2015, p. 166); that is, cultural forms, references, and practices in intercultural communication are emergent. There could also be awareness that language, culture, and communication are not 'correlated and tied to any single native speaker community or even group of communities' (Baker, 2015, p. 166).

The ICA model is selected here for its rejection of solely nation-based concepts of cultures and languages and recognition that a language such as English is not bounded to particular communities of users (Baker, 2015). It conceives that the cultural forms, practices, and frames of reference are not fixable in a priori categories for intercultural communication but are adaptive and emergent in communication. Therefore, ICA emphasises the unpredictable, dynamic, and context-specific character of intercultural communication, and recognises the role of ELF/EMF as based on the needs of particular moments of communication. It is also relevant to a rejection of assumptions that intercultural learning is most effective following interactions with local individuals who represent the 'target' for learning (among students and institutions). The components are in broad rather than rigid categories and can accommodate varied individual interpretations and understandings of intercultural learning. The presentation over three levels could suggest a linear developmental progression from basic to advanced, to intercultural awareness; however, the model's author notes that the components are not necessarily linear and that individuals could display aspects of a particular level at one point and then another level at other points (Baker, 2015). As individuals gain a deeper understanding of these components following varied learning experiences, each component may be enhanced and strengthened. For example, an individual may demonstrate a basic understanding of culture as a set of shared behaviors, beliefs, and values, but following some experience/learning (e.g., using English in intercultural communication during student exchange), they may gain a deeper understanding of the role culture and context play in any interpretation of meaning. This might fall within level one, but it represents learning within that level. I argue that ICA offers a dynamic and flexible approach to intercultural learning that can recognise the multicultural and multilingual realities of individual exchange communication and learning experiences.

The ICA model's relevance to education has been examined in a growing number of empirical studies, including Baker's (2015) in Thailand, Yu and van Maele's (2018) in China, Kusumaningputri and Widodo's (2018) in Indonesia, and Abdzadeh and Baker's (2020) in Iran. These studies have suggested development typically occurs between levels one and two in educational settings. In relation to short-term student exchanges, ICA has been investigated among Japanese university students in Humphreys and Baker's (2021) study, where some development was also observed between levels one and two. Findings from these studies support ICA as a framework for understanding intercultural learning in terms of fluid understandings of culture and language and their relationship in intercultural communication.

3 Intercultural and Global Englishes Education

3.1 Introduction

In Section 3, I expand the discussion on ELF/EMF and global English-language use and offer a basic comparison of traditional English-language and intercultural education with contemporary educational approaches, which I relate to student exchanges.

3.2 Global Englishes and Multilingual Communication

In a relatively short time, the number of English users has grown from an estimated 5 to 7 million speakers in the seventeenth century to the global language it is today (Jenkins, 2015b). Driven in particular by British colonialism, US influences, and population changes, it is estimated that now one in three people can communicate to some degree in English (Crystal, 2008). While there are other international languages, English is dispersed more widely in international contexts, is used in a wider range of domains, and hence there is considerable cultural diversity among its users (Dewey, 2007). Today, more than 80 per cent of global English users are estimated to be non-native users (Sharifian, 2013, p. 2), and as a result, most global English use takes place among non-native users in multilingual contexts of communication. These changes are reflected in contemporary frameworks of understanding, including World Englishes (WE; e.g., Kachru, Kachru & Nelson, 2006), which concerns documenting varieties of English, identified and defined within linguistic and geographic models. The WE framework is influenced by Kachru's (1982) three-circle classifications: the 'inner' circle, where English is spoken as a 'native' language; the 'outer' circle, where it is spoken as a second language in locations where it may have (or may have had) some official status; and the 'expanding' circle, where it has no official status and is learnt as a 'foreign' language. The WE framework does not stress that one variety is better than another, but that all varieties are to be respected (Salih & Omar, 2021). This three-circle model has been highly influential in improving awareness of diversity in English use, contributing to a shift in perspective towards English language ownership (i.e., that it belongs to all users; McKay, 2018). For exchange students, knowledge around WE is relevant for awareness of diversity in English use. Additionally, it can help to challenge conventional and native speakerist notions of language ownership.

ELF/EMF (see also Section 1.2.3) offers an interaction-based framework for understanding diversity in English use and variability in communication. In recognition of the multilingual aspects of communication involving English, the definition of ELF has been expanded from the use of English among speakers of different linguistic backgrounds to 'English as a multi-lingua franca', or EMF[3] (see Section 1.2.3; Jenkins, 2015a). Essentially, EMF is a multilingual activity where individuals utilise multilingual resources, including linguistic and non-linguistic resources, in communication where English is among the available contact options (but not necessarily used; Ishikawa, 2021). In multilingual ELF/EMF settings (e.g., during certain student exchange experiences), communication can involve individuals drawing on integrated resources, linguistic or otherwise, to negotiate meaning in communication (i.e., EMF, or translanguaging; Li, 2018). ELF/EMF considers variation in interactions as more complex than implied by geographic boundaries, as well as involving a fluid negotiation of meaning in communication, irrespective of membership to a particular

---

[3] ELF is retained here for its links to associated research, though EMF is the preferred term.

'circle' (Jenkins, 2015b). Indeed, the unlimited variability in its use is beyond what may be standardised (Seidlhofer, 2011). Both WE and ELF/EMF are represented by GE (see Section 1.2.3), a broad term inclusive of research and practices in these connected areas (Rose & Galloway, 2019). Awareness of GE themes and practices, in particular ELF/EMF, is important for exchange students in terms of understanding the flexible and negotiated nature of language use in multilingual contexts.

These multilingual realities of English use are typically absent from educational practices (e.g., Rose & Galloway, 2019). Instead, there remain tendencies to treat English use in binary terms of 'correct' and 'incorrect', with standard normative 'deviations' as errors to be fixed (Jenkins, Cogo & Dewey, 2011). As a result, these 'errors' can be allocated significant time in classrooms, even when they are not an 'obstacle to communication success' (Seidlhofer, 2003, p. 18). Such practices are particularly found among, and informed by, 'language authorities' (e.g., codified written grammar, language guides, and language testing) and they can also be seen in classroom practices, driven by teacher beliefs (Hynninen & Solin, 2017, p. 270). Learning experiences within these conventional practices may lead students to form perspectives about the requirements of effective language use as based solely on the use of standard norms (Mayumi & Hüttner, 2020). While traditionally, conceptions of norms are based on notions of 'standard' language use, they can also be based on common language use within particular linguistic communities or corpus-based understandings of local communication practices (Hynninen & Solin, 2017). In other words, by analysing language use in a corpus, insights can develop to inform normative understandings of what constitutes 'correct' or 'proper' language use within a community. In multilingual communication contexts (including many exchange contexts), English-language use is not stable enough for representation by codified norms or corpora regularities, and so norms are socially negotiated in individual language practices (Hynninen & Solin, 2017). This negotiation involves the creative use of multilingual resources in flexible communication, with such resources emergent in communication in response to particular situations. In exchange contexts, students may be required to negotiate language use in flexible and emergent ways; therefore, an understanding of the creative use of multilingual resources can be crucial for communication experiences during exchanges.

3.3 English Language and Culture in Educational Approaches

In teaching, standard normative understandings are evident in language-as-code approaches to grammar and vocabulary learning (i.e., grammar translation), which emphasise the translation and memorisation of words and grammatical rules based on assumptions that there are direct equivalents in first languages. Communicative language teaching, which offers an alternative to structural grammar-translation, is now preferred in many national language policies and in local educational management (e.g., in syllabus and curriculum design; Karakaş, 2021). It prioritises speaking and listening and includes a communication focus to vocabulary study (i.e., words not taught in isolation on lists as in structural approaches). Alongside communicative language teaching, influential theoretical frameworks of communicative competence have been developed to outline how communication goals are achieved in ways considered 'socially appropriate' in communication with standard native users (e.g., Bachman, 1990; Canale, 1983; Canale & Swain, 1980). In both communicative teaching and theory, however, focus tends to be on interactions with native speakers (as 'authentic' users) in which 'appropriate' use is defined by the (imagined) standard norms of 'inner circle' countries. Such educational practices can be found in policies and curricular design guided by the Common European Framework of Reference, which outlines competencies for language use, and they can be found in widely used testing systems (e.g., IELTS, TOEFL, TOEIC). As described in Section 2.4, the influence of native speakers is also found in certain exchange educational practices.

Contemporary pedagogical frameworks represent diversity in English language and reject native speakers as the target for teaching/learning. These frameworks include the teaching of WE-informed ELT (Matsuda, 2017), which represents non-standard norms in classroom practices and attempts to legitimise variation in English. This framework incorporates the diversity of English usage around the world, moving away from standard English norms. A related approach is ELF-aware pedagogy (Sifakis, 2019), involving teachers engaging with ELF research to form their own understandings by critically reflecting on their local teaching situations. The aim is for teachers to become aware of language and language use, instructional practice, and learning, and how ELF could be integrated within teaching practices. ELF-aware pedagogy emphasises an understanding of the realities of ELF and for this knowledge to be used to inform teaching practices that are relevant and inclusive for learners from diverse linguistic and cultural backgrounds. Relatedly, Global Englishes Language Teaching (GELT; Rose & Galloway, 2019) aims to inform how ELT curricula can be developed in a shift from traditional ELT to GE-informed ELT. These aims include focusing learning and language ownership on all English users, not only native English users, and moving away from standard norms as the guide for learning towards an understanding of English use in diverse and multiple forms. GELT also promotes a fluid understanding of cultures for learning, beyond target (i.e., 'inner circle') cultures. These three frameworks share a common goal of promoting a more inclusive approach to ELT beyond a narrow focus on standard norms. They advocate for a greater appreciation of linguistic diversity and variation and highlight the importance of contextual factors and local teaching situations in shaping language learning and teaching. They are relevant to exchange students in culturally and linguistically diverse settings in their representation of a wider range of English speakers.

Transcultural language education (Baker & Ishikawa, 2021) is a pedagogical framework that also rejects idealised native speaker communication models, with learning processes incorporating awareness of multilingualism and EMF. This framework integrates culture in language education in ways that go beyond national cultural framing, and it proposes an integration of ICA for intercultural learning. It also highlights intercultural citizenship as the target for learning alongside its rejection of native speaker targets. Transcultural language education challenges conventional approaches in which culture is treated as belonging to, and shared by, people in distinct and homogenous groups. On this basis (in traditional educational practices), cultural meanings become essentialised as learnable aspects of knowledge (McConachy, 2018). These approaches, however, do not account for differences in how meaning may be represented and interpreted among individuals or how individuals are unlikely to share identical characteristics within a sociocultural context. Practitioners should, however, understand that no one model is appropriate for all contexts at all times and that many teachers (myself included) adopt different practices based on particular needs (Baker et al., 2022). Indeed, there are moments when curricula and local educational management decisions necessitate that I work in more established ways.

These contemporary frameworks can be used to inform curricular developments for student exchange learning (e.g., language classes, exchange events, project work, programme add-ons). In addition, they can be used in the design of pre-exchange learning innovations. In such innovations, incorporating some recognition of cultural variation in classes or learning materials can provide interesting content in relation to exchange destinations; however, education should also focus on building awareness of diversity among individuals and help them foster connections with other individuals and other communities (intercultural citizenship; see Section 3.4). While educational support in the pre-sojourn period is crucial, in certain contexts it is inadequate or restricted only to practical matters, or conveyed through lectures that might not facilitate active engagement with learning materials (Jackson, 2020). In terms of language use, the development of pre-sojourn awareness of ELF/EMF – important given the potential convergence of multiple languages during exchanges – can help students build connections with other individuals during exchanges. Efforts to prepare students can also draw upon existing approaches, such as the Intercultural Education Resources for Erasmus Students and their Teachers (IEREST, 2015). IEREST offers a comprehensive set of teaching resources for supporting intercultural learning and the personal growth of students prior to, during, and following their overseas exchange experiences. These kinds of educational innovations can help to ensure that students are prepared for their exchanges and can make the most of opportunities overseas. They can also support students on their return to home universities by helping them reflect on their intercultural learning experiences and formulate new learning goals (Holmes, Bavieri & Ganassin, 2015; Messelink, van Maele, & Spencer-Oatey, 2015).

3.4 Student Exchanges and Intercultural Citizenship Education

Education for student exchanges (i.e., pre-departure training, exchange programme design, and post-sojourn support) can also be informed by intercultural citizenship education (Byram, 2008), a framework for helping students to develop responsibilities towards individuals and multicultural communities. Byram (2008) refers to characteristics to outline how education may help individuals reflect on their experiences towards individual changes (p. 187):

1. Causing/facilitating intercultural citizenship experience, and analysis and reflection on it and on the possibility of further social and/or political activity, i.e., an activity that involves working with others to achieve an agreed end;
2. Creating learning/change in the individual: cognitive, attitudinal, behavioural change; change in self-perception; change in relationships with Others (i.e., people of a different social group); change that is based on a particular culture but related to the universal.

In intercultural citizenship education, 'citizenship' refers to 'a subjective sense of belonging to communities at a variety of levels – the local, regional, national, transnational or global level' (Barrett & Golubeva, 2022, p. 78). It is not based on connections with communities of native language users or national cultural members (i.e., how language should be used, and how people should act). The aim is to facilitate educational experiences towards individual changes in intercultural knowledge, skills, and attitudes in order to be active in multicultural communities, where there are diverse perspectives and practices (Wagner & Byram, 2018). Community, therefore, connects to collaboration within multicultural groups (e.g., a group of exchange students of different backgrounds). Learning/change occurs from collaborating within these communities in ways that challenge any existing cultural perspectives in favour of new international ways of thinking and acting (i.e., international identifications). It is in interacting with others within these multicultural communities that individuals can develop social identities through connections with others (Byram et al., 2017). In a simplification of development processes, student reflection on new ideas and perspectives within a multicultural community leads to changes in perspectives towards 'common sense' (i.e., how to act in particular situations); students then change how they act by developing new actions (and new perspectives towards 'common sense') within these communities (Byram et al., 2017). This could involve, for example, a group of international students working together on a student exchange or online exchanges in which students discuss global issues, with examples of action including writing articles for local publications, presentations in school settings, or video presentations (Byram et al., 2017).

In past studies, critical intercultural perspectives developed in a classroom project involving interactions between Argentinian and British students, highlighting the role of interaction for intercultural citizenship development (Porto, 2014). Other past studies have uncovered complexity around the student understanding of intercultural citizenship (Golubeva, Wagner & Yakimowski, 2017) and that more systematic education would be effective in a context of internationalisation policies around developing global identities (Han et al., 2017). Intercultural citizenship has also been found to be limited in some study abroad classroom instruction, and more understanding and experience can develop outside classrooms (Fang & Baker, 2018). These studies highlight the importance of interaction and critical reflection in fostering citizenship among students, both inside and outside of the classroom. Moreover, since experiences abroad often involve variable English use (e.g., Mocanu & Llurda, 2020), emphasising ELF/EMF in multilingual contexts links to intercultural citizenship in their shared aims to promote respectful interaction with individuals from diverse cultural and linguistic backgrounds. Opportunities to develop intercultural citizenship can, however, be somewhat limited on short exchange experiences, and it is also unlikely to happen just because students meet other people. It needs to be integrated within, for example, project work where international students of different backgrounds collaborate, or in extracurricular activities that can provide further opportunities to build on organised project work or other educational experiences (Fang & Baker, 2021). Indeed, it could be possible for informal activities to result in intercultural citizenship, including, as Baker and colleagues (2022) state, 'leisure times with international friends, movie nights, music, travelling, cooking, dining in dormitories, and volunteering projects' (p. 5).

4 Case Study: Connecting the Themes in the Japanese HE Context

4.1 Introduction

I now connect themes I have discussed in a case study of the experiences of fifteen Japanese students, drawing on reports of their individual trajectories through exchanges and particular contextual variables during programmes overseas. To provide context, I first outline aspects of HE internationalisation in Japan and local institutional practices. I then present my findings and interpretations.

4.2 Background: HE Internationalisation and Student Exchange in Japan

Since the 1980s, educational internationalisation has been prominent in Japanese education ministry guidelines (Gottlieb, 2008). In these guidelines, internationalisation is closely linked to the English language, based on its perception as the language required for engagement in the global economy (Eades, Goodman & Hada, 2005; Yamagami & Tollefson, 2011). At the secondary level, policies tend to be prescriptive and focused on English-language study, while at the HE level, limited government intervention implies that internationalisation initiatives are the responsibility of individual institutions and teachers (Yonezawa, Akiba & Hirouchi, 2009). Within Japanese universities, it is now common for international offices to be established and staffed by international centre directors and administrative staff (Oba, 2011, cited in Yonezawa, 2017, p. 378). Initiatives vary according to particular institutional conditions and there are different interpretations of how to support internationalisation among individuals involved. In some Japanese HE settings there is also a lack of clarity regarding internationalisation, including, as Vickers (2018) states, 'confusion over what 'internationalization' means, why (or even whether) it matters, who it is for, and with whom it should engage' (p. 1). The common focus of institutional efforts is on quantitative increases of international students and staff, but, as noted in Section 2.2, such measures do not capture the complexity of internationalisation in educational practice (Brotherhood, Hammond & Kim, 2019). There are also views that numbers-based approaches to internationalisation are used to cover slow-to-occur actual educational reform in Japan (Poole, 2016).

These institutional efforts to increase numbers stem from the belief that a diverse student and staff population, including native English-speaking teachers, will provide intercultural interactions and contribute to student understanding and tolerance of diversity (Whitsed & Volet, 2011). Nonetheless, there are perspectives in Japan (and elsewhere) that the recruitment of international faculty can be used to create an image of internationalisation based on a need for universities to be 'seen to do something' in terms of HE internationalisation (see also Section 2.2; Stewart & Miyahara, 2011, p. 69). These attempts can be problematic, since, as Brown (2019) states, the 'peppering Japanese academe with foreigners, particularly those who are not Asian' can be perceived as tokenistic attempts to address internationalisation (p. 405). Many international faculty (including English communication teachers) do not work in full academic departments, and as such, tend to be peripheral members within institutions (Oda, 2018). Furthermore, support for international faculty has been documented as lacking in Japanese universities (Huang, 2009), and many international teachers are not themselves directly involved in internationalisation initiatives beyond involvement in language teaching (Whitsed & Wright, 2011).

In language learning centres, international teachers are employed to teach English communication classes in 'international' learning centres where students typically study English as a requirement rather than choice. However, including 'international' in the name of a learning centre can be awkward for claims relating to 'international' or 'global', widely used terms in Japanese institutions, particularly if only one language (English) is being taught (based on fixed standard norms of particular Anglophone settings by native English teachers representing particular 'inner circle' national cultures). On ELT practices, standard language-oriented approaches remain common despite statements in national policies that English to be taught should not be biased towards English spoken in specific regions by specific groups (MEXT, 2017). This treatment of the English language is particularly evident in curricula and teaching practices in secondary-level language grammar-translation teaching for university entrance exam preparation (Humphries & Burns, 2015), which has 'set the standards for English study in Japan' (Stewart 2009, p. 10). Preparing for these entrance exams is an essential feature of secondary ELT (Tanaka, 2010), around which high-school English teachers present grammatical rules and vocabulary for translation, usually based on textbook readings (Sakui, 2004). Indeed, the influence of these entrance exams is significant as roughly 50 per cent of high-school graduates take these in order to go on to university education (Sugimoto, 2003, p. 119). Despite the influence of university entrance exams on educational practices, studying for these exams has been connected to a low motivation to learn English among many students in Japan (Kikuchi & Sakai, 2009), and there are reports that many students do not engage with English beyond the context of these entrance exams (Whitsed & Wright, 2011). At the university level, institutions tend to decide their own curricula, often incorporating English language programmes as compulsory adjuncts for non-language major students within separate independent centres alongside their main degree programmes in established and full university departments.

International exchanges are important aspects of HE internationalisation in Japan, though there also tends to be a quantitative focus on increasing participation rates over educational outcomes (Koyanagi, 2018). In 2011, the Council for Promotion of Human Resources for Globalization Development was established to encourage institutions to develop exchange opportunities (Yonezawa, 2017), and accordingly, most universities in Japan now offer exchange options (JASSO, 2018). Although the pandemic affected recent levels of participation in exchanges (76 per cent drop in numbers between 2019 and 2020 (Japan Association of Overseas Studies, 2021)), promoting international exchanges has been a policy priority, with an expanded government budget for participation and scholarships, including for short-term student exchanges. In 2004, the Japan Student Services Organization (JASSO), an independent administrative institution affiliated with the education ministry, set up new scholarships to fund exchanges from eight days to three months (JASSO, 2022). Consequently, there was an increase in the number of programmes offered, and JASSO (2018) reported that 96,641 students took part in 2016. However, the majority of programmes were shorter than one month, including trips of just three days provided the trip was for research, intercultural experience, or language study (McCrostie, 2017). Specific projects established and funded by the Japanese government include Japan Revitalization Strategy, Go Global Japan Project, Inter-University Exchange Project, and the TOBITATE! Young Ambassador Program (Ota, 2018). Policy emphasis is on international cooperation and building a global outlook among graduates around language and intercultural skills for active work in international contexts, commonly referred to in the Japanese contexts as 'global human resources' (Sugimura, 2015). This emphasis aligns with the objectives of intercultural citizenship.

4.3 Research Methods

4.3.1 Research Questions

In this case study, I explore the exchange experiences of fifteen Japanese university students by addressing two research questions:

1. What are the factors in students' trajectories through short-term student exchanges that offer experiences leading to intercultural learning and changes in perspectives towards English use in intercultural communication (in line with GE)?

2. To what extent did short-term student exchange experiences support intercultural learning (ICA and intercultural citizenship) and changes in perspectives towards using English in intercultural communication?

The aim of question one was to develop understanding around how programmes of different character led to differences in intercultural learning and awareness of GE-related themes, in particular ELF/EMF; that is, contextual factors contributing to development, such as variations in programme type, length, and types of social contact. The aim of question two was to investigate intercultural learning that individuals experienced during student exchanges, including a focus on changes in perspectives towards using English in intercultural communication. The study looked at any changes over time by comparing items from student interviews across the longitudinal research period (pre-exchange, post-exchange, and six months later), examining individual perspectives and experiences. The focus of this study is, therefore, on students' reports of educational practices in both the home university and on student exchange programmes, and on any changes in individual students' perspectives.

4.3.2 Research Context

The case study was conducted at a non-language major university at which particpation in short-term international exchanges and English language learning were promoted in institutional internationalisation policy. The English department provided two ninety-minute mandatory English communication classes each week for first- and second-year students. A prescriptivist standard normative approach could be identified in the curriculum (mainstream ELT resources, certain online resources, many teacher-developed materials, assessment systems) and in many teacher perspectives (based on personal observations). However, use of ELF/EMF could be observed in communication with students, particularly in a designated open common discussion area within a self-access centre. Based on my own experiences teaching in the context, the majority of students' English level and motivation were low. In university reports regarding alumni, most did not go on to use English or work in international contexts. The exchange programmes were managed by administrative staff in an international exchange division, established in 2015, and involved short-term experiences in diverse locations, including language study, research study, cultural exchanges, and study tours. Table 2 provides a picture of the university's recent participation rates in short-term student exchanges (the decline is due to the pandemic).

The aims of exchanges in the setting (extracted from the university website) included: 'gain a global perspective through overseas experience'; 'become

Table 2 Recent participation in student exchanges
at the university

Year	Number of participants in student exchanges
2017/18	242
2018/19	273
2019/20	266
2020/21	0
2021/22	1

independent'; 'experience different ways of living and thinking in different cultures'; and 'develop a flexible mind'. Developing global human resources as a goal of exchanges was also explicitly acknowledged, with definitions in the setting around 'ability to act and fulfil an active role in Japan and the world, with the flexibility to collaborate from both local and global perspectives'. I argue that intercultural citizenship is relevant to these statements, though assumptions about ideal interactions (i.e., with local native speakers) were evident in advertising material for exchange programmes offered by the university (see Section 2.4).

4.3.3 Participants and Their Exchanges

The fifteen students who contributed to this study took part in exchanges in the 2017/18 academic year were, at the time, current or former students in the English learning centre. The interviews in this case study were conducted during that time. Differences among these students included gender (eight female students, seven male), age range (nineteen to twenty-four), past international experiences (five with, ten without), programme duration (seven days to one month), as well as different types of programmes and destinations offered in the university's exchange options. In Table 3, I have included information about the fifteen students and their selected programmes (all names are pseudonyms).

To provide context on these students' programmes and motivations, they reported that their main objectives for taking part in student exchanges were to improve their English communication skills and establish international connections. Following exchanges, students reported varied individual experiences. I interpreted broad patterns in the experiences of different programmes from their accounts. Noriko, Mariko, Sayaka, Kodai, Kaori, Tomo, Takeshi, and Miki were enrolled on research-based or language study programmes conducted on international campuses where they interacted with other international students.

Table 3 Fifteen students and their exchange programmes

Name	Sex	Age	Year of study	Exchange programme	Length	Past study overseas?
Noriko	F	21	2	Research-based, Germany	1 month	N
Mariko	F	21	2	Research-based, Germany	1 month	Y
Yuki	M	19	1	Cultural & study tour, Malaysia	10 days	N
Masa	M	19	1	Cultural & study tour, Malaysia	10 days	N
Sayaka	F	21	2	Language study, Poland	3 weeks	N
Mayu	F	21	2	Cultural tour, US	10 days	N
Ryota	M	21	2	Cultural tour, US	10 days	N
Daichi	M	21	3	Cultural tour, US	10 days	N
Miki	F	24	5	Research-based, Hong Kong	1 month	Y
Kaori	F	19	1	Language study, US	3 weeks	N
Kiyoko	F	21	2	Cultural tour, Taiwan	7 days	Y
Minami	F	21	2	Cultural tour, Taiwan	7 days	Y
Kodai	M	20	1	Language study, UK	3 weeks	N
Takeshi*	M	23	3	Cultural tour, US	10 days	N
Tomo*	M	21	3	Language study, Philippines	1 month	Y
				Cultural tour, US	10 days	
				Language study, US	1 month	

* Takeshi and Tomo took part in two exchanges which are both represented here.

Yuki and Masa took part in cultural and study tours in Malaysia, which involved time on culturally and linguistically diverse international campuses. Among these students, multicultural and multilingual aspects were significant in students' reports. Mayu, Ryota, Daichi, Kiyoko and Minami participated in chaperoned group tours, organised by the home university, where opportunities to use English in intercultural communication were limited. Takeshi and Tomo participated in programmes in this grouping, but also referred to other exchange experiences in the interviews. Although the distinction between 'study' and 'tourism' experiences was somewhat ambiguous in faculty-organised and chaperoned tours, these programmes were classified as official overseas study programmes by the university and are therefore included in this study. This variation is explored in depth in the findings in Section 4.4.

4.3.4 Data Collection

The research aimed to provide a complex and in-depth description of students' engagement in intercultural communication and intercultural learning during their exchanges. As such, it is focused on a qualitative and interpretive understanding of individual processes of learning and changes in perspectives, acknowledging that statistical measures might not fully capture individual and subjective perspectives (Silverman, 2014). It is, therefore, in line with a research trend towards qualitative research on individual trajectories through international study experiences (Coleman, 2013; Kinginger, 2009). The study combined interviews at three points (pre-sojourn, post-sojourn, six months later), observations (institutional practices, student learning practices), and documentary data (website statements, exchange promotional material, ELT materials and resources).

In the semi-structured interviews (which I conducted), I looked at these students' exchange experiences in terms of ICA, understandings of GE (in particular around ELF/EMF), and how intercultural citizenship could be identified in students' reports of educational practices and individual learning motivation through their exchange trajectories (i.e., pre-, during, and post-exchange). The interviews lasted thirty minutes on average. While interview guides were utilised, the participants were given flexibility to discuss areas of personal importance pertaining to the research areas (Silverman, 2014). In the initial interviews, a rapport was established, foundational topic areas were covered, and impressions of the students' perspectives were formed to be compared with later responses. The second interview allowed for greater individualisation and centered on the exchange experiences themselves. Follow-up questions and an exploration of unresolved and interesting emergent points were the focus of the final interviews. Participants had the option of responding in either Japanese or English, depending on their preference. I arranged translations, where necessary, and a bilingual co-worker verified the accuracy of the translations against the original texts. The inclusion of English language in certain interviews is a methodological limitation and may have restricted the comprehensiveness of some student responses. Nonetheless, the transcripts/ translations were presented to the students at the conclusion of the data collection period, with an invitation for them to contribute additional thoughts on the research area, in either English or Japanese. Any feedback received could be included in the analysis. Translations are identified where they appear in the findings.

Background observational and documentary data were obtained through a process of participant observation involving observing and documenting practices in the educational setting (Silverman, 2014). In particular, I looked at institutional educational practices (curricula, learning resources), student exchange support mechanisms (provisions of learning support), individuals (including students, teachers, and international department staff, following informal interactions), and documents (as noted above). I took notes to record these data and note my own interpretations.

4.3.5 Data Analysis

In the analysis, I looked for changes in the students' perspectives in how they talked about culture and language in intercultural communication through the data collection. I treated 'perspectives' as related to subjective viewpoints or opinions that may be shaped by personal experiences and background, but which may change after experiencing subjective events (e.g., intercultural communication during exchanges). In later interviews, I looked for examples of students reframing their perspectives towards language and culture. The interviews might not have provided objective 'facts', but they offered particular representations of perspectives and experiences in a dialogue with me, as the interviewer/researcher (Byrne, 2004). All data were transcribed and analysed using NVivo 11, with predetermined codes based on the conceptual areas; however, data-driven codes were also allowed to emerge given flexibility in the interviews (Miles, Huberman & Saldaña, 2014). This coding approach ensured there was a conceptual closeness to the research areas, with an openness to new directions (Silverman, 2014). A thematic framework developed from analysis of the interview data, which involved continuous adjustments to reflect emergent data. Although the number of participants was small, the study aimed to build detailed individual accounts to document their experiences, with cross-participant comparison used to identify common thematic threads (Silverman, 2014). Findings are constructed representations of what was shared in the interview contexts as well as items from other data sources. I have attempted to be transparent in my positioning, in my approach to these topic areas, and my management of a research process. As the interpretation of the findings and the implications drawn from them are subjective, readers are encouraged to engage with the data and my interpretations and draw their own conclusions based on their own perspectives and experiences.

4.4 Pre-exchange Experiences of Culture and English Language Learning

4.4.1 Pre-exchange Learning Experiences: Culture

The fifteen students recalled past culture learning experiences from school and ELT (including at the current university context) in ways that implied national fact-based cultural learning in cross-cultural comparisons between Japanese and other national cultures. Kaori (interview 1) stated: 'In high school, we did a project about food and lifestyle … I learnt about differences between Japan and Canada.' Similarly, Tatsuya (interview 1) reported: 'I did an English project about American culture and Japanese culture … I learned that we are different.' Such reports of culture learning were common among these students. These experiences of culture learning, reported in the first interviews, did not appear to link to the educational attempts to support international ways of thinking (i.e., intercultural citizenship).

4.4.2 Pre-exchange Perspectives: Culture

In the pre-exchange interviews, there were instances of essentialism among the participants relating to the basic cultural awareness in ICA level one. For example, Ryota (interview 1) generalised individuals within his own national culture in a comparison with a generalised understanding of individuals in the United States: 'Japanese people are very shy ... American people are more active.' In a similar example, Daichi (interview 1) talked about his experience with an American teacher, contrasting levels of 'tension' with Japanese individuals: 'His tension was very high but Japanese people's tension is not high, so we were very tired.' In a further example, when talking about what he had learned about culture, Kodai shared a basic surface-level cultural perspective around facts (interview 1): 'In Japan, toilet and bathroom is divided but in Canada, same place.' In my observations, the interviews did not reveal broad awareness of complexity of culture, though some students likely found nation-based labels as relevant in the interviews in response to the questions asked.

4.4.3 Pre-exchange Learning Experiences: English Language

Regarding ELT experiences, there was an emphasis on English-language learning as a subject of knowledge rather than learning towards communication. Students provided similar reports of secondary ELT experiences around reading and grammar-translation study and preparation for university entrance tests. Nine students explicitly reported few opportunities to use English at secondary level, illustrated by Miki (interview 1), who stated: 'I have to speak perfect English because in high school we have to study about grammar or sentence not speaking ... we only study to pass test so I think English is just a subject.' I also interpreted connections between English study and obligation to develop English communication skills, though there were perspectives towards learning English as difficult and unnecessary in Japan given its limited use in many contexts. Tomo illustrated this point (interview 1): 'When I was in high school, I wasn't interested in English at all, but I study English to enter university ... I can do anything without English in Japan and there is little person who speak English, so I don't need it.'

4.4.4 Pre-exchange Perspectives: English Language Use

Pre-exchange, most students associated authentic English use with standard normative correctness, expressed by Sayaka (interview 1): 'I want to learn

American English because it's correct English.' This perspective was also evident in negativity towards local teachers, including from Mariko (interview 2): 'Japanese teacher can't teach correct English.' Perspectives towards 'authenticity' as based on standard normative understandings may have been formed during the ELT experiences and practices described by these students, for example Miki in interview 1: 'My teacher corrected all my mistakes ... I believed I had to speak correct English.' Similarly, Tomo (interview 2), when looking back to past ELT experiences, stated: 'I studied from textbooks and used to believe English was just one' (also indicating a changed perspective towards English use; see Section 4.4.7). The standard language preferences also implied an absence of ELF/EMF awareness; however, some basic WE-based awareness was indicated around location-based differences in English use within the 'inner circle', though other uses tended to be grouped under 'non-native'. For example, Kaori (interview 1) reported: 'Australian English is different to British English ... so difficult ... I prefer American English ... I don't want to learn non-native English.'

4.4.5 Pre-departure Institutional Support

Institutional support was reported by the students as limited to the provision of basic information and it did not appear to include clear specifics about programmes, as Noriko (interview 1) mentioned: 'International centre do only the paperwork ... I didn't get much information.' In pre-sojourn learning advice, students reported that the international division had advised them to research information about their destination national cultures. Based on reports, this advice was not focused on any potential for learning through interaction with individuals in multicultural environments. Kiyoko (interview 2) reported: 'The university told me to learn something about the culture in Taiwan, that's all.' Moreover, the institution did not clearly differentiate between programme types; as a result, several students were unclear about aspects of their programmes or what constituted study, illustrated by Yuki (interview 2, translation): 'My image of studying abroad was a bit like a travel ... I'd like to make a clear distinction between them next time.' Based on these students' accounts, I interpreted that pre-sojourn institutional practices were not pedagogically based according to the conceptual orientation of this research, which also relates to assumptions of intercultural learning occuring automatically on stays abroad.

4.4.6 Student Motivations for Exchange Participation

Most students reported motivation to develop 'global' identities during student exchanges, illustrated by Ryota (interview 1): 'I want to study abroad because

I want to be global . . . I can speak to foreign people and learn new things. It will be hard to do that in Japan.' Yuki (interview 1, translation) expressed a similar motivation alongside a view that achieving this aim in Japan would be difficult: 'I want to place myself in an environment where I cannot use Japanese. I want to explore what kind of culture or perspective exists outside Japan and hope to utilise the experience in future.' Therefore, there were implied expectations that international exchanges would lead to intercultural learning and the formation of a 'global' identity in contexts in which a reliance on the Japanese language was not possible. This motivation was linked by students to English use. For example, Noriko (interview 1) said: 'Many Japanese people think we should study English because Japan is becoming a global country . . . I hope to become a global person.' However, 'global' also tended to be linked to national cultural understandings, as shown by Mayu (interview 1): 'I want to see abroad [global] views so this project is I learn American's culture.' Thus, understandings of 'global' and 'intercultural' among students appeared vague, at least in how they were shared in the interview contexts. While students were motivated to use English, there was also nervousness, illustrated by Noriko (interview 1): 'I feel scared, and I worry that I can be understood in English, and if I can make friends if I make mistakes.' Such trepidation could be linked to language learning experiences focusing on the 'correctness' of standard norms and limited past experience using English in communication.

4.4.7 Student Exchanges: Multicultural and Multilingual Experiences

Social Contact and International Connections. Some students (Noriko, Mariko, Sayaka, Kodai, Kaori, Tomo, Takeshi, Miki, Yuki, and Masa) characterised their experiences in terms of cultural and linguistic diversity among other students with whom they connected. There were examples in these students' reports of acknowledging the particular nature of their encounters with individuals of diverse background, and identifying some commonalities. For example, Kodai (interview 2) stated: 'I study with Morocco, Colombia, Korea, Italy, Turkey, Pakistan, France students . . . my class friends talked to me a lot so I can practise my English skill and learn about them . . . when we worked together I found we had a lot in common.' Among these students, there were also reports of informal social activity with other students. Takeshi (interview 1), in reference to a language study programme in the Philippines, talked positively about opportunities to interact with a diverse range of individuals using English. He said: 'It was so good experience for me to speak English. I could get so many friends . . . I can understand and feel there are other people.' For students on such programmes in culturally and linguistically diverse campuses, there were also opportunities to organise their own time, allowing them to build relationships with other international students in social settings, illustrated by Miki (interview 2) – 'I had a lot more free time to plan my time with friends' – and Tomo (interview 3) – 'In Houston, I could make my own plans to go out in the evenings with friends.'

Intercultural Learning. Among these students, there were reports of new intercultural learning formed through connections made during their exchanges. For example, Mariko (interview 2) stated: 'In Germany I got used to speak to a lot of people. I learnt a lot of new things from them, and I want to use their ideas in the future.' Similarly, Yuki (interview 2, translation) reported learning new ideas through interaction, and motivation to incorporate them in his own thinking: 'I interacted with Malaysian and international students . . . I talked about the way people think, hobbies or relationships. I learnt new ideas and I want to absorb them . . . I felt a connection with those people.' As illustrated by Mariko and Yuki, students on these programmes appeared to accept new ideas encountered in multicultural contexts and expressed a motivation to use these new ideas in the future (though the extent to which they did so is unknown). Based on connections in a multilingual environment, there were examples of new confidence using English in such learning, illustrated by Miki (interview 2) on her research-based programme at an international campus in Hong Kong:

> I became confident talking with many people . . . they are not mother language, so I think it's easy to understand compared to American people . . . we change what we say to help each other . . . In Japan, many people think it's good to be quiet in class but in Hong Kong many students asked the teacher questions. It was interesting because many students could share and then learn more . . . I asked some questions too . . . I got more confident after speaking English at the university. I learned to try to do many things by myself.

Miki analysed and reflected on an intercultural experience and adapted to a multicultural community by acting on that reflection and speaking up in class. Miki's experience appeared to contribute to a change in confidence. I also interpreted reflection and change, building identifications within a multicultural community from Noriko's account (interview 3): 'Study abroad gave me a new perspective . . . I learnt a lot from working with other students and I started to think differently when I was with them.'

Changing Views towards English Use. While in pre-sojourn perspectives there was a tendency to associate authentic English use exclusively with native English speakers, students percieved experiences engaging with variability in English use on their programmes as meaningful. For example, Kodai (interview 2) reported hearing new accents and using English with other international students (and was enthusiastic about building new international friendships): 'English pronunci-ation was different, and I was surprised … I talked a lot, and I could feel difference between them … I want to make more abroad friends, so I want to go again.' Similarly, Noriko observed the importance of listening to different English pronunciation to improve her own listening skills, not focusing on native English users (interview 2): 'I want to hear a lot of English pronunciation … I need to hear more from many countries' English. My listening will become better if I hear more pronunciation.' These students reported an interest in further exposure to different uses of English, with pronunciation as the main area in which differences were talked about, as perhaps they were more easily identifi-able as differences among these students. Changes in confidence were also evident across the accounts of students on these types of exchange, including Mariko (interview 2), who stated: 'I could speak to many people. I think I'm a little more confident with my English now.' It also emerged that some students were more comfortable talking to other international students, as illustrated by Takeshi (interview 2): 'When I speak with native English speaker, I feel a little pressure to speak very well but when I talk with non-native speaker, I feel more relaxed. English is not native language for them and it's same to me. Their English is not perfect, and mine too.'

In an illustration of longitudinal changes in perspectives towards English use, Kodai indicated changes occurred after his experience on a three-week language programme in London. Prior to his sojourn, he had spent time playing online games, using in-game chat features to communicate in English with players from Thailand (interview 1): 'Sometimes I play internet games and then I communicate with foreign country people in Thailand … they are not correct.' Post-sojourn, Kodai (interview 2) expressed some positivity towards non-native English use, based on positive experiences socialising with a diverse group of classmates: 'I got to talk to people from various countries … they have their own accents and expressions. I was genuinely glad I could learn those things.' It implied that Kodai developed more awareness of differences in English use and accepted diversity rather than defining variability as 'not correct', as in the first interview.

Developing ELF/EMF Perspectives. There was also an indication of changes towards accepting and using ELF/EMF in communication, as Noriko (inter-view 2) implied: 'Sometimes I changed my explanation so if I say something difficult, I explain it different.' In addition, Tomo (interview 3), after an exchange experience on a multicultural campus in the United States, reported shifting a view towards ELF/EMF: 'I chose Houston I wanted to meet new people different cultures … before I went to USA, I thought grammar is very important, but some people talk a lot, but their grammar is not correct but if I change, we can communicate each other and learn about each other.' Similarly, Takeshi indicated use of ELF/EMF during his exchange in a multilingual setting in Philippines. He remarked (interview 3): 'I learned to focus on communication and not using perfect grammar or pronunciation.'

Longitudinal development of ELF/EMF perspectives is illustrated by Masa, who took part in a cultural tour to Malaysia involving time interacting with individuals on a culturally and linguistically diverse campus. He had not been abroad before and described his past English experiences as limited. Pre-sojourn, he was negative towards his own English and reported little confidence using English (interview 1, translation): 'Because I think my English is bad. I thought I could speak more confidently if my English skills were better.' Following his sojourn, Masa (interview 2, translation) indicated a changed view in favour of using English, noting that communication could be effective following a more flexible and less norm-regulated approach: 'I noticed when I changed what I said, or didn't worry about what I said, they could understand me ... it felt good to talk with them ... they were not native speakers but they were better than me.' Masa accepted 'non-standard' English use among others, but not his own; however, later he reflected again on his English use and reported more confidence (interview 3, translation): 'I could learn they can still understand my badly pronounced English, so it made me want to go overseas even more.' Therefore, such experiences of intercultural communication on culturally and linguistically diverse campuses supported new ELF/EMF perspectives and included engagement in ELF/EMF in intercultural communication, though there was negativity towards own English use.

4.4.8 Student Exchanges: Focus on Target Culture and Language

Target (national) culture learning was more evident on faculty-led, group exchanges, as interpreted from thematic connections in the students' accounts of their exchange experiences. Some students on these programmes (Mayu, Ryota, Daichi, Kiyoko and Minami, as well as Takeshi and Tomo in reference to other exchange experiences) had objectives to use English in communication with local (native English) students and develop a 'global' perspective. For example, Daichi (interview 1) stated: 'I would like to be a global person ... I hope to make new American friends and learn from them' (see also Section 4.4.6). However, there were few opportunities to achieve this through interaction, as Takeshi (interview 3) remarked: 'I'm not satisfied. We didn't have enough opportunity to talk to American students ... it's difficult to make friends in so few minutes.' Limited social contact with others was also a source of frustration for Ryota (interview 3), who had wanted to connect with local individuals: 'I couldn't send my heart to American people.' Moreover, there was criticism towards wide use of Japanese and towards organisational decisions restricting independence, illustrated by Tomo (interview 3): 'I don't have any chance to speak English ... almost [all] time we talked in Japanese ... We don't have to do anything by ourselves because [chaperone] do everything.'

These programmes included organised communication events and cultural exchanges involving student presentations on aspects of Japanese culture to students overseas. However, these presentations did not appeal to students, as Daichi (interview 2) demonstrated: 'We did a performance about origami ... I just explained origami but it's not interesting.' In addition, Takeshi (interview 3) shared his experience of these events: 'I talked about kimono, but it's not my inspiration.' Based on such comments, it implied that these students desired more substantial intercultural learning experiences, apparently aware that interactions during these organised events were superficial. Among these students, there was also a tendency to report on differences among individuals encountered during these cultural events at national levels without expressing commonalities among individuals (i.e., ICA level one). For example, Daichi (interview 2) reported: 'American people were different to us. They are friendly but sometimes they said things that are confusing to us.' In addition, some students on these programmes reported negative intercultural experiences following organised communication activities, relying on stereotypes in their descriptions. For example, Ryota (interview 3): 'It was a little difficult to talk to him ... he said interesting thing, but I didn't agree. I think Japanese people is more kind.' Kiyoko (interview 3) provided a further example of generalising individuals: 'Taiwan people are more confident, and Japanese are more shy.'

Students on such programmes also expressed negativity towards experiences using English, in which notions of standard normative language use remained influential in the accounts and there was no indication of new ELF/ EMF understandings or changes in communication practices. For example, Minami (interview 2) stated: 'Taiwanese English is not so good, but they try to speak ... I'm careful for grammar and pronunciation so I couldn't speak.' Daichi also commented on language use (interview 1): 'American people speak English correctly. Sometimes it was difficult to understand them ... It made me understand that I have so much to learn to communicate like them.' In addition, there was self-criticism towards students' own language use, and willingness to accept blame for communication breakdowns. For example,

Mayu (interview 3) stated: 'They spoke so fast, it was hard to understand. But they are using English correctly. I have to practise more.' These experiences, therefore, did not appear to support new ELF/EMF perspectives.

4.4.9 Post-exchange

On returning from exchanges, students were required to write a report and deliver a presentation for study credits as part of formal post-sojourn requirements at the university, reported by Tomo (interview 2): 'I did presentation about America trip and culture about the hotel and food after coming back.' I observed that these presentations tended to involve descriptions of basic information about organisational aspects of the programmes and cultural generalisations about the host countries. The students reported that educational direction was not provided to help students unpack their experiences. For example, Sayaka (interview 2) reported: 'I made presentation with my friend . . . I didn't get help.' Despite internationalisation statements on the university website around developing global perspectives from student exchanges, these post-sojourn educational practices appeared focused on fact-based culture learning rather than on intercultural perspectives. Post-sojourn, there were student claims of greater motivation to engage in intercultural learning; however, other university concerns obstructed how this motivation translated into new learning practices, illustrated by Minami (interview 3), who stated: 'I want to learn more about different cultures . . . but I have to do many tests this year so it's hard to use the self-access centre.' Motivation to study English was also expressed in the post-sojourn period, including by Yuki (interview 2, translation): 'I hope to create English sentences on a daily basis, such as keeping a diary or translating conversations . . . I haven't been able to do so because of my studies.' Mariko (interview 2) also reported difficulties: 'I'd like to learn about English but now I'm doing experiments, so I don't have time.' Extending learning was, therefore, affected by other commitments, limiting the extent that potentially important learning could be consolidated or built on post-sojourn.

4.5 Individual Intercultural Learning

Focusing in-depth on ICA learning with reference to intercultural citizenship, I selected four students (Mayu, Yuki, Noriko, and Miki) based on individual differences and representing different programme types. This focus enabled a more in-depth analysis of ICA learning compared to a larger sample (some data excerpts in this section can also be found in Humphreys and Baker's (2021) study). For each student, I first include a profile before presenting data and a discussion next to interview excerpts from the three interviews (pre-departure, within a month of return, and six months later).

4.5.1 Mayu

Profile. Mayu, a twenty-one-year-old third-year biology student, took part in a ten-day faculty-led US cultural tour alongside twenty-three other students from the home university. Mayu reported motivation to use English in intercultural communication and develop an intercultural identity through communication with individuals from the local destination community. The tour involved university and high-school visits where the students presented on aspects of Japanese culture to local students, followed by brief and staged communication exchanges. As stated in Section 4.4.8, complaints emerged towards organisational aspects of the programme, including around a lack of independence, rigid schedules, and few opportunities to use English in intercultural communication. Pre-departure, Mayu was active in the university's self-access centre, regularly using English in communication with teachers.

Interview 1: I want to see abroad views, so this project is I learn American's culture. I will visit university and high school because I do presentation on Japanese culture. My group topic is educational snack ... American students are interested in Japanese culture.

In interview 1, Mayu reported motivation to participate in her exchange to learn 'America's culture'. While this may be based on challenges expressing her perspective in the interview context, it also implied a basic understanding of culture at the national level, without talking about differences among individuals. She also talked about culture in general terms (as she did in later interviews) in comments linked to awareness of 'culture as a set of shared behaviours, beliefs, and values' (level one), based on her generalisation of culture.

Interview 2: The truth is [I did] three presentations in high school and university ... this project is not recommended because schedule ... We can do nothing, we don't have time to meet people ... American students are very interested in politics, but we are not interested.

In the second interview, Mayu talked about her required presentation (on educational snacks; i.e., common snacks some students enjoy during periods of study). She had expected presentation content would appeal to local students in these cultural exchange events (interview 1); however, in such practices, there were risks of promoting learning around national-level cultural differences. This kind of activity did not imply connections would form with others in line with intercultural citizenship. Mayu complained about the programme timetable and organisation, and about not having time to connect with local students. In a report of communication with students during these events, Mayu relied on a basic comparison between those she talked to, and a shared Japanese perspective (as she saw it) around a lack of interest in politics. This perspective may also be associated with level one awareness of 'others' culturally induced behaviour, values, and beliefs and the ability to compare this with our own culturally induced behaviour, values, and beliefs'.

Interview 3: I want to know a variety of cultures. So, because, like food is very difficult. Many people, many countries, I like food, so I want to know many countries food.

Later, Mayu reported motivation to engage in further culture learning, though she continued to focus on surface-level aspects of culture, connected with level one. She talked about culture in general understandings as shared in the behaviours, beliefs, and values of members of particular communities.

4.5.2 Yuki

Profile: Yuki was a nineteen-year-old first-year engineering student who participated in a ten-day cultural tour to Malaysia. He was accompanied by seven other Japanese students and a professor from the home university. The programme included several days working and socialising with other international students on a culturally and linguistically diverse university campus. The group stayed in a university dormitory on campus. Yuki reported spending time with Malaysian, Chinese, Indian, Sudanese, and Turkish students. It was his first time overseas. He opted to take part in the exchange based on his interest in learning new ideas from individuals outside Japan. He reported few past experiences using English outside formal classroom settings. All interviews are translations.

Interview 1: I also always wanted to go abroad. Also, I heard that experiencing foreign cultures and learning different perspectives would change my own way of thinking.

In the pre-exchange interview, Yuki expressed motivation to learn new ways of thinking and an expectation that they would influence his understandings of culture. It implied interest in developing an international identity through connection with others. He was open to new intercultural experiences and appeared willing to develop new understandings. Yuki grouped culture under the label 'foreign', implying a basic comparison-based understanding of national cultures, which, in the analysis, I linked to awareness of 'others' culturally induced behaviour, values, and beliefs and the ability to compare this with our own culturally induced behaviour, values, and beliefs' (level one).

Interview 2: It was normal that things were different. When I came across different customs, I tried to ask someone about it, think about it myself and understand. Even in Japan there are people who have different styles. I tended to keep a distance from those people, but I started making efforts to approach these people.

On return, Yuki reported awareness of differences among those he interacted with on the international campus, observing differences among people as 'normal', indicating learning about other perspectives and accepting these perspectives, connecting with intercultural citizenship. Yuki also reported a change from formerly avoiding cultural differences to seeking out differences during his sojourn. He reported engagement in processes of personal reflection when he encountered some perceived difference, linked in this research to level two awareness of 'others' culturally induced behaviour, values, and beliefs and the ability to compare this with our own culturally induced behaviour, values, and beliefs'. Yuki also expressed a recognition of diversity among individuals in Japan; that is, awareness of 'individuals as members of many social groupings including cultural ones' and 'multiple voices or perspectives within any cultural grouping' (level two). It implied that his characterisation of identity went beyond national descriptions on recognition of differences among individuals.

Interview 3: Mindset towards others. It became less frequent to feel like 'Why they can't understand?' and I became able to embrace unexpected, new ideas from others.

In the final interview, Yuki talked about adapting to new ideas encountered overseas, which connected with his pre-sojourn objectives, indicating a successful exchange experience. As he 'embraced' new ideas, it implied there was fluidity in his intercultural communication experiences as he responded to requirements of interactions and adapted to new perspectives. This flexibility in communication may be linked to level two awareness of 'cultural understanding as provisional and open to revision'. Yuki apparently delinked language, culture, and individual identities; thus, in his account, ICA learning was observed from level one towards a more intercultural position in level two. It may also link to re-examining existing ideas following connections he made overseas, informally in a multicultural community (an aspect of intercultural citizenship). Particular experiences afforded by his programme that allowed him to socialise with others in a culturally and linguistically diverse environment appeared to offer intercultural learning experiences that he perceived as personally meaningful.

4.5.3 Noriko

Profile. Noriko was a twenty-one-year-old female third-year pharmacy student who spent a month in Germany on a research-based project alongside other international students, also on a culturally and linguistically diverse campus. English was used there in formal and informal settings. She conducted a short pharmacy-related research project on the programme under the supervision of English-using German teachers. She was joined by one other student from her home university. The host institution arranged all programme content, including add-ons, and provided accommodation in student apartments. In addition to pharmacy-specific learning, Noriko was motivated by opportunities to develop her English skills, communicate with individuals on her programme, and develop 'global skills', as she put it. She was socially active on her programme, reporting new friendships with individuals from a range of backgrounds. Prior to her sojourn, Noriko regularly utilised the home university's self-access centre to engage in communication with teachers, though she reported few experiences of intercultural communication outside the university setting. It was her first time abroad.

Interview 1: Some American people are very kind, and they laugh at my jokes very much. But in case of England people, they didn't laugh at my jokes. For example, so, fly soup joke that I did to Tom, he didn't laugh at it, and he asked what mean . . . I freeze. However, in case of American people Daniel or Sam, they laughed at that. So, it's different between American and England.

In the pre-exchange interview, Noriko indicated a basic conceptualisation of culture in generalised comparisons between British and American people, without commenting on individual differences within national groups, and treating individuals and their national cultures as inextricably linked. She also emphasised cultural differences over commonalities connected to level one awareness of 'culture as a set of shared behaviours, beliefs, and values'.

Interview 2: We did a lot of work together and talked about it after classes . . . When I talk with foreign people, I could learn new things. It's very new thing, it's interesting and sometimes the culture . . . sometimes foreign countries knowledge is not similar to us and it's strange . . . That knowledge gave me new ideas and sometimes it broke my obstacles. So, I like talking with people and I like to observe those foreign countries' culture.

Post-sojourn, Noriko talked about group activities she was involved in and was positive about learning new things from 'foreign' people. Noriko also referred to similarities and differences in a cross-cultural comparison between Japanese people ('us') and foreign people (singular 'they'). She connected her own thinking and behaviour to members of her own national group in the use of 'us', indicating (in a moment of the interview) awareness of 'our own culturally induced behaviour, values, and beliefs and the ability to articulate this' (level one). However, there also appeared to be a shift in her perspective indicating acceptance of differences and awareness of 'others' culturally induced behaviour, values, and beliefs and the ability to compare this with our own culturally Induced behaviour, values, and beliefs'. Her apparently diverse intercultural experiences during her exchange in formal and informal settings indicated enhanced within-level development of ICA in understandings of later components in level one. There was also indication of intercultural citizenship development, of new ideas formed in a multicultural community breaking 'obstacles' and providing new perspectives.

Interview 3: I have thought about my study abroad a lot . . . So, for example, I'm Japanese, so I know about Japanese. I work, or I play, with Japanese moral and I, we, think or consider about something with Japanese ethics. However, foreign people do the same. So, in Germany, people think about something with Germany ethics or moral. As a result, sometimes the fundamental thing is different. Sometimes I think the idea will be the opposite.

In the final interview, Noriko indicated further reflection on intercultural learning experiences during her exchange. She talked about different 'ethics' among individuals, and how people from different cultures consider ethics from their national perspectives; that is, awareness of 'our own culturally induced behaviour, values, and beliefs and the ability to articulate this' and 'others' culturally induced behaviour, values, and beliefs and the ability to compare this with our own culturally induced behaviour, values, and beliefs' (level one). This comment also implied rethinking notions of common sense according to different individuals, formed during experiences in a multicultural community during her exchange. However, Noriko continued to rely on national understandings without talking about differences among individuals within settings (i.e., level one, in my interpretation).

4.5.4 Miki

Profile. Miki was a twenty-four-year-old fifth-year student on a six-year pharmacy course. She spent a month on a research-based programme at a university in Hong Kong where she studied herbal medicine under the supervision of a local teacher in English in a similarly diverse environment as Noriko. She stayed in a hall of residence with other students. Miki attended the programme independently. She was motivated to participate based on research activities, using English, and learning from others in an international setting. As a second-year student, she took part in a language study programme in the United States. Comparing the two experiences, she reported more independence on the Hong Kong programme and a more controlled experience in the United States alongside other Japanese students. In Hong Kong, she studied and socialised with other international students and reported several social experiences.

Interview 1: Sometimes when I talk with foreign country people, they have very interesting thinking, I think. So, I want to talk with many foreign country people, and I want to know many thinking.

In the first interview, Miki reported a desire to connect with new people and learn new ideas and perspectives. She was enthusiastic about opportunities to gain new intercultural experiences. Her use of 'foreign country people' and 'interesting thinking' also implied awareness of 'others' culturally induced behaviour, values, and beliefs and the ability to compare this with our own culturally induced behaviour, values, and beliefs' (level one) and 'the relative nature of cultural norms' (level two).

Interview 2: I think there are no students who didn't speak in the class. I think it was very interesting, as I said, students could share many questions . . . We did some projects together, for example interviewing students activity . . . People were different to what I thought. I was surprised sometimes because they said things I didn't expect. I learnt new ideas from what I thought . . . I became confident talking with many people . . . they are not mother language, so I think it's easy to understand . . . we change what we say to help each other.

In the second interview, Miki talked about perceived differences in classroom behaviour among other international students, linked to awareness of 'the relative nature of cultural norms' (level two). Miki went on to talk about differences she observed among people she interacted with on her international campus as unexpected, which I linked to awareness of 'cultural understanding as provisional and open to revision' (level two), also mentioned in Section 4.4.7. Educational experiences in project work alongside others in a multicultural setting indicated some intercultural citizenship development around reconsidering her pre-existing perspectives in favour of new thinking, after time in a multicultural environment.

Interview 3:   The most thing is I was talking with many people in English. I could talk with many people in English. I could talk with people I didn't know, and I got confidence to talk with many people of different nationalities . . . They all taught me different things.

Six months later, Miki reported positively on her intercultural communication experiences and connections she formed with other students on her programme. These encounters appeared to support ICA learning, as she identified that individuals she spent time with were influenced by diverse factors, consituting an awareness of 'multiple voices or perspectives within any cultural grouping' (level two) from which she could learn as her confidence grew. It also indicated flexibility towards emergent communication practice. She expressed a view that communication with other language students was easier and that students adapted what they said, when necessary, to ensure there was understanding in particular moments in communication. Based on such language use, Miki was able to learn different things from those she was around. In her account, ICA learning may be seen as within level two, from awareness of 'the relative nature of cultural norms' in the first interview to awareness of 'cultural understanding as provisional and open to revision' later (i.e., enhanced level two learning). Miki appeared to enjoy her experience and perceive meaning from engagement with diversity among the individuals with whom she connected. She remarked she had learnt 'new ideas' from those she connected with in a multicultural community during her exchange.

4.6 Key Findings

I now summarise the key findings outlined in Sections 4.4 and 4.5, presented in a bullet-point format and accompanied with references to their locations in the findings, in order to help readers locate more detailed information.

- In students' past culture learning, national fact-based learning was evident in approaches characterised by cross-cultural comparisons (Section 4.4.1).
- In pre-exchange student perspectives, there were mainly examples of basic cultural awareness in relation to ICA level one (though students may also have found the use of national labels appropriate to the interview contexts; Section 4.4.2).
- In past educational experiences, English language was handled as a subject of knowledge for exam study. There was limited focus on communication and few opportunities to use English in practice, as well as perceptions that English learning was difficult (Section 4.4.3).

- In pre-exchange perspectives, authenticity in English use was associated with standard norms. Awareness of ELF/EMF was not indicated, though some awareness of variety-based differences was evident (in terms of standard 'inner circle' differences; Section 4.4.4).
- Pre-departure institutional support involved the provision of basic logistical information. Learning advice centred on target culture learning, with learning potential from interactions in multicultural and multilingual contexts not featuring in pre-departure advice (Section 4.4.5).
- Motivation to participate in student exchange was based on developing 'global' identities, linked to English use. There were expectations that exchange contexts themselves would lead to intercultural learning, which tended to be understood around national cultural understandings. Anxiety about using English during exchange may be linked to past language learning experiences focusing on standard notions of 'correctness' and to student perspectives towards authentic English use solely in association with native English users (Section 4.4.6).
- Social contact and engagement, as well as organising own time independently, in culturally and linguistically diverse contexts led to new international connections (Section 4.4.7).
- International connections formed in multicultural and multilingual contexts led to new intercultural perspectives. There was an indication of intercultural citizenship experiences in building identifications with others in multicultural communities (Section 4.4.7).
- Students perceived engagement with variability in English use as meaningful. There were new perspectives towards English use beyond standard notions of 'correctness' and new confidence using English (Section 4.4.7).
- Communication experiences in multilingual contexts led to new ELF/EMF perspectives (though at times accompanied with self-criticism towards own English use; Section 4.4.7).
- Target culture and language learning was evident on faculty-led, group exchanges. Opportunities to develop a 'global' identity were limited based on few intercultural communication experiences. The few chances for students to be independent and organise their own time were criticised by students. There was a tendency among these students to express basic cultural awareness associated with ICA level one, and no changes in perspectives towards English use in intercultural communication were observed (Section 4.4.8).
- Post-sojourn support was not provided to help students identify learning taking place on their sojourns. Reports of greater motivation to engage with intercultural and English learning were obstructed by other university responsibilities (Section 4.4.9).

- Target-culture, group tour programme design provided few opportunities to connect with individuals overseas and support non-essentialist intercultural learning. Expressions of basic awareness of culture involved linking individuals as inseparable from their national cultures (Section 4.5.1).
- Following fluid intercultural communication in multicultural and multilingual communication settings, new intercultural perspectives developed, including the disconnection of language, culture, and individual identities, associated with ICA level two. Additionally, there was a connection with intercultural citizenship based on social contact in culturally and linguistically diverse settings (Section 4.5.2).
- Diverse intercultural communication experiences in formal and informal settings can support ICA learning, including within-level ICA learning. Experiences in multicultural communities formed during exchanges may help students reflect on, and rethink, cultural perspectives, and accept new ideas (Section 4.5.3).
- Connections formed in a multicultural and multilingual setting supported ICA learning. Engagement with diversity in a multicultural community led to some connection with intercultural citizenship (Section 4.5.4).

4.7 Research Question 1

4.7.1 Pre-exchange

Short-term student exchanges are popular (JASSO, 2018; Perry, Stoner & Tarrant, 2012) and they are important aspects in relation to HE internationalisation (e.g., Killick, 2015; Knight, 2008). It is therefore necessary to explore various aspects of these experiences in trajectories through exchanges, including pre- and post-exchange experiences and perspectives. As the students indicated in their responses, past experiences of culture in learning were handled in cross-cultural educational approaches around shared knowledge, traits, and characteristics among people from named national cultures (Section 4.4.1). However, such representations of culture as a set of factual information specific to particular national communities simplifies and essentialises cultural meanings as learnable knowledge (McConachy, 2018), and has been widely critiqued in intercultural educational practice (e.g., Baker & Ishikawa, 2021; Scollon, Scollon & Jones, 2012). Such representation is, I argue, unlikely to prepare students for the varied intercultural communication experiences during student exchanges, which are more dynamic and complex than in these traditional educational representations.

Pre-exchange perspectives towards English-language use appeared to be influenced by past language learning experiences and a focus on standard norms

(Section 4.4.3; see also Mayumi & Hüttner, 2020). These influences were particularly evident in the curricula and teaching practices of secondary-level language grammar-translation teaching for university entrance examination preparation (e.g., Humphries & Burns, 2015). Students reported limited past learning focus on communication and few past opportunities to use English in practice (Section 4.4.3). It was understandable, then, that prior to going abroad, students were anxious about using English. Motivations for participating in student exchanges centred on developing 'global' identities and intercultural learning, which the students linked to English language use (Section 4.4.6), and which reflect how English and internationalisation are linked in Japanese national educational policies (Eades, Goodman & Hada, 2005; Yamagami & Tollefson. 2011). While there were expectations that exchange contexts would automatically lead to intercultural learning and opportunities to use English in intercultural communication among the students, there was a tendency to conceptualise this learning around national cultural understandings in the pre-exchange period (Section 4.4.1).

Reports of pre-departure institutional support mechanisms did not reveal a provision of any intercultural learning support initiatives, contradicting the university's website statements on intercultural learning and internationalisation, as well as neglecting the important role of pre-departure support (see Section 4.3.2; e.g., Jackson, 2020). Furthermore, there did not appear to be comprehensive institutional examination into the quality of intercultural learning or intercultural communication provided by specific experiences; as a result, there were gaps between the expectations and realities of exchange learning, institutionally and among participants (see Koyanagi, 2018). These gaps may also relate to assumptions of overseas learning as leading automatically to intercultural learning in the context of HE internationalisation, though as noted, such learning is not guaranteed (Jones, 2017). Some students were unclear about differences in programme types and what constituted study (Section 4.4.5), reflecting related research perspectives on the lack of distinctions between programme types (Engle & Engle, 2003). Moreover, the advice given to students emphasised learning about the target (national) culture, without considering the potential benefits of interacting with people from diverse linguistic and cultural backgrounds. This advice did not take into account the opportunities for learning that arise from engaging in multicultural and multilingual contexts.

4.7.2 Exchange Experiences

Students who participated in sojourns in culturally and linguistically diverse settings experienced more substantial intercultural learning and developed new perspectives towards using English in intercultural communication, consistent with ELF/EMF (Section 4.4.7; Jenkins, 2015a; Seidlhofer, 2011). In contrast, group exchanges led by faculty members tended to focus on target culture learning, but opportunities for intercultural communication were limited. Students on those programmes did not report any changes in perspectives towards using English in intercultural communication and tended to express only basic cultural awareness associated with ICA level one (Section 4.4.8; Baker, 2011). These experiences were characterised by wide use of Japanese and limited socialisation outside the group, as aspects almost built into the design of these kinds of programme. This design is problematic for intercultural learning occurring through interaction with others (e.g., Cubillos & Ivento, 2018), and students are unlikely to encounter new ideas or perspectives (Isabelli-García, 2006). While short programmes may be easy to set up in group tours, they do not always provide time for students to engage in new educational settings or form meaningful relationships with others. These kinds of experiences may still be perceived by students as important, but here the students criticised these programmes for having few chances to connect with others and few opportunities for independence. Indeed, many student complaints were focused on organisational factors around providing minimal exposure to English and engagement with others (Sections 4.4.8 and 4.5.1). These exchange practices, then, did not match students' motivations to develop international connections and intercultural perspectives (see also Mitchell, McManus & Tracy-Ventura, 2015). The findings suggest that target culture and language practices in group cultural tours, despite the ambitions of these programmes around intercultural learning, are unlikely to meet the intercultural learning goals of HE internationalisation.

In the students' pre-departure aspirations, there was a preference to learn from teachers who were native English speakers and engage only with native English users (Section 4.4.4). However, these aspirations did not reflect the learning potential from ELF/EMF use as realities of exchange programmes. Students also reported motivation to participate in exchanges around developing 'global' identities, though this was vague in students' understanding. It appeared to link primarily to English-language learning (i.e., global identity = speaking English; Section 4.4.6). This equating of a 'global' identity with speaking English (based on standard norms) risks reinforcing the dominance of native English speakers in educational practices. On language use, standard language practices were evident in target-language approaches involving simplistic connections (in student motivations and institutional expectations) between 'inner circle' standard uses and authenticity (Section 4.4.8; see also Trentman & Diao, 2021). Students saw speaking English as a way to access intercultural learning opportunities and participate in international multicultural communities, but there was a lack of awareness of multilingualism in exchange settings. Thus, the complexity and diversity of English use in different contexts, as well as the role of ELF/EMF, were not features of any new learning about English use, as reported by the students on these types of programmes (i.e., faculty-led group tours). However, among students on experiences in culturally and linguistically diverse settings, there was evidence of changes in perspectives towards English use, and a recognition of its complex and diverse nature, as well as the role of ELF/EMF (see discussion in Section 4.8).

4.7.3 Post-exchange

There was a lack of comprehensive post-sojourn educational opportunities, which may have impacted the students' ability to identify intercultural learning that took place during their experiences (see Holmes, Bavieri & Ganassin, 2015; Messelink, van Maele, & Spencer-Oatey, 2015). There was also a tension between students' motivation for post-exchange learning and other university obligations, which could undermine the perceived benefits of internationalisation through exchanges provided by universities Additionally, the extent to which students reported new post-exchange motivations was affected by university demands outside of the exchange contexts, further highlighting a mismatch between stated internationalisation policies and educational practices. There is a clear need for universities to provide comprehensive support for students before, during, and after their exchange programmes to fully realise the benefits of these experiences.

4.8 Research Question 2

4.8.1 Pre-Exchange Perspectives: Culture and English Language Use

Pre-exchange perspectives among the students were largely based on surface-level understandings of culture (at least in how they were shared in the interviews; Section 4.4.2). These included several examples of basic awareness of culture linked to ICA level one (Baker, 2011). For some students, essentialist comments were observed in their accounts throughout data collection, in relation to how students conceptualised language and culture in communication (Sections 4.4.8 and 4.5.1). Such essentialist perspectives in the pre-exchange period may impact on how students engage in meaningful intercultural communication if it limits the extent to which they adapt to cultural diversity. In facilitating intercultural learning through interaction, I have argued that there is a key role of language (though, as noted, it is often minimised in research [Baker & Ishikawa, 2021]); hence, I have integrated an additional focus on perspectives towards English language use. In the research, authenticity in English use in association with standard norms and awareness of ELF/EMF was not indicated in the pre-departure interviews, though some awareness of variety-based differences was evident (particularly in terms of 'inner circle' differences; Section 4.4.4). This association of authenticity in English use in students' pre-exchange perspectives may limit their ability to engage in meaningful intercultural communication in multilingual contexts where variable English use goes beyond this narrow conception of 'authenticity'.

4.8.2 Intercultural Awareness

After engaging in social contact and interaction in culturally and linguistically diverse contexts, some students experienced new learning towards ICA level two (Baker, 2011). Specifically, international connections formed in multicultural and multilingual environments were found to be effective in promoting such shifts towards level two (Section 4.4.7). For example, Yuki's experience on a multicultural campus led to a disconnection of language, culture, and individual identities towards perspectives associated with level two (Section 4.5.2), and Miki indicated within-level two learning (Section 4.5.4). Indeed, within-level development was significant for some students, at levels one (Section 4.5.3) and two (Section 4.5.4). The research suggests that smaller ICA learning can occur within particular levels, representing enhanced learning within particular levels. However, other students' accounts were coded at level one following experiences in programmes characterised by target culture and language learning, and few intercultural communication opportunities, as interpreted from the interview accounts. These findings suggest that a focus on the fluidity of cultures and languages in communication through exposure to diverse perspectives, as provided on multicultural programmes, is more effective for ICA learning than the more essentialist approaches characterising other exchange experiences. The findings are also consistent with Baker's (2015) assertion that ICA learning is not necessarily smooth or linear, and individuals may display aspects of a particular level at one point and then a different one at another point.

4.8.3 Intercultural Citizenship

The study demonstrated that engaging with culturally diverse communities during exchanges, especially through social interactions (Section 4.4.7), encouraged international identifications that could be associated with intercultural citizenship. As noted, intercultural citizenship is a significant objective of international education (Killick, 2015), and is in accordance with the notion that such identifications can develop through interactions with individuals from diverse cultural backgrounds in multicultural communities, even if these communities are temporary (Byram, 2008). In particular, students who engaged in collaborative activities within multicultural communities reported changes in their intercultural perspectives, with some displaying a connection with intercultural citizenship (Section 4.4.7). For example, Noriko (Section 4.5.3) reflected on, and rethought, her past cultural perspectives, while Yuki also formed connections with others in a temporary multicultural community during his exchange (Section 4.5.2). Additionally, Miki's engagement in a multicultural community led to a basic connection with intercultural citizenship as she learnt new ideas following reflection, accepting and adapting to new perspectives (Section 4.5.4). As students engage with diversity in these settings, they are exposed to new ideas, perspectives, and practices, which can lead to shifts in their intercultural perspectives and identities. New ways of thinking and acting with an international perspective were not, however, present among students on other programmes. The findings suggest that some connection with intercultural citizenship is possible with particular exchange experiences and can be more clearly linked to HE internationalisation goals.

4.8.4 Changing Perspectives towards English Use in Intercultural Communication

As noted, ICA acknowledges the functional needs of intercultural communication regardless of cultural or linguistic background (Baker, 2015). It does not rely on preconceived notions or stereotypes associated with specific cultures or ways of using language, and it recognises intercultural communication beyond cultural or linguistic differences. By acknowledging the functional needs of intercultural communication, ICA recognises that individuals adapt to specific contexts and requirements of communication situations, taking into account the diverse perspectives and communication practices that may be involved. ICA learning on multicultural and multilingual campuses was accompanied by new confidence in using English in multilingual settings (Section 4.4.7). Changes in perspectives were interpreted in some accounts towards the use of English in intercultural communication (i.e., awareness of diversity beyond standard uses, accepting and using ELF/EMF). As noted in particular contexts, and as in related findings, there were extensive socialisation opportunities with other international students (e.g., Schartner, 2016). The findings suggest that when students engage in intercultural communication on such campuses, they develop new perspectives on English language use, particularly with regard to ELF/EMF (Section 4.4.7). These perspectives align with research emphasising fluid negotiation of meaning in communication, in which language practices are independent of one's membership of a particular 'circle' of language users (Jenkins, 2015b). Some students indicated flexibility in their use of English, beyond adherence to standard norms, in order for communication to be successful. This included changing language structures and repeating or rephrasing statements (Sections 4.4.7 and 4.5.4). There were perceptions among students that communication with other international students was more equal than communication with native language users (e.g., Csizer & Kontra, 2012). This shift in perspective towards English language use is a crucial outcome for exchange students as it shows how confidence in using English can increase following communication experiences in multilingual contexts (Section 4.4.7). Short-term student exchange experiences can therefore lead to new perspectives on using English that reflect the realities of its use in global contexts, despite the influence of pre-sojourn ELT experiences on students' language perspectives evident in the pre-exchange period.

The study also revealed that students on faculty-led and home university-organised group tours did not develop a deeper understanding of the potential of ELF/EMF. Indeed, these students had only superficial contact with others during their sojourns. The lack of contact with target native speakers (see also Baker-Smemoe et al., 2014), which was evident in certain exchange reports (Section 4.4.8), led some students to express feelings that their exchange experiences had on some level been a failure, as found in related research findings (Çiftçi & Karaman, 2018). The study highlights the importance of addressing native-speakerist perspectives in exchange practices in ways consistent with the contemporary pedagogical frameworks discussed in Section 3.3 (Matsuda, 2017; Rose & Galloway, 2019; Sifakis, 2019), in particular transcultural education (Baker & Ishikawa, 2021).

5 Recommendations and Conclusion

5.1 Introduction

Based on interpretations from the case study, I now present recommendations for research in Section 5.2 and recommendations for programme design and pre-departure and post-sojourn support in Section 5.3. To address points made in the findings in relation to the conceptual area, I outline a series of practical learning activities in Section 5.4. I then conclude the overall Element.

5.2 Recommendations for Research

Firstly, case-driven qualitative research can be particularly effective for examining the individuality of overseas study experiences (Coleman, 2013; Kinginger, 2009). The application of qualitative methodologies can also support collaborative engagement among both researchers and participants towards more in-depth insight in this research area than available in large-scale quantitative research applying particular developmental models. The use of such models, I have argued, can constrain the 'measurement' of any learning according to their own fixed categories of analysis (see Section 2.4). Qualitative exchange research may also more effectively capture the unique differences between individual experiences and highlight specific contextual variables that are significant to individual students. Rather than treating contexts as fixed, such research can be used to recognise the significant variety among contexts and how exchanges may be experienced differently by students.

Throughout this work, I have contended that intercultural communication during student exchanges can be a complex and dynamic process that involves fluid negotiation of meaning and interaction between individuals from different cultural and linguistic backgrounds. Frameworks used to analyse intercultural learning should be flexible to capture the diverse and fluid nature of these interactions, as well as understandings of conditions on particular programmes that contribute to learning. The ICA model offers an important resource for this purpose as it recognises the common use of ELF/EMF in unpredictable intercultural communication, and it moves away from national cultural orientations. Its components are deliberately general to accommodate diverse individual experiences as well as understandings of particular conditions in exchange programmes that contribute to learning. The twelve stages may suggest a linear developmental trajectory, but ICA is not a model for assessing student progress as they move through these stages, since the stages are abstractions, and individuals may, in different moments, demonstrate higher levels and then 'revert' to earlier points in other moments (Baker, 2015). Its broad categories and adaptability to diverse contexts make it an effective tool for understanding complex individual experiences in intercultural learning. It is particularly useful for exchange research because it acknowledges the fluidity and unpredictability of intercultural communication, and it provides a flexible framework that can be adjusted to a variety of experiences and conditions, thus enabling a deeper and individual understanding of intercultural learning outcomes. To develop understandings of ICA in relation to student exchanges, there is a need to apply it in further research to a wider range of exchange experiences.

I have also emphasised the multicultural and multilingual aspects of international exchanges as important in how participants connect with, and learn from, other international students (see also Csizer & Kontra, 2012; Schartner, 2016). The role of ELF/EMF is crucial for many effective intercultural communication experiences where English language use is delinked from defined geographic boundaries according to particular standard norms in multilingual communication contexts. The use of ELF/EMF in intercultural communication in such contexts is also common (e.g., Mocanu & Llurda, 2020), and student exchanges, as evidenced in Section 4, can play an important role in promoting recognition and acceptance of variability in English language use. It would be useful to develop new research to help identify effective ways to promote awareness of ELF/EMF among exchange students. Importantly, such research should acknowledge the multicultural and multilingual character of exchange experiences where communication involving English goes beyond standard language practices. In addition, there is a need for more research on intercultural citizenship, including further investigations into factors that contribute to or hinder this development in multicultural and multilingual settings, as well as how to maximise the potential for a connection with intercultural citizenship through programme design and new educational innovations. There are opportunities in research to examine how these areas can support the needs of exchange students in a wider range of exchange contexts, particularly in research on new educational innovations in these areas, which may be useful to a wide range of practitioners.

5.3 Recommendations for Practice

5.3.1 Programme Design

To design effective short-term exchange experiences, it is important to align exchange learning with the expectations of students and the internationalisation goals of universities. Students often have specific goals and interests in mind when participating in exchange programmes, such as intercultural learning and using English in intercultural communication, which need to be represented in exchange learning experiences. Specific internationalisation goals that universities hope to achieve through their exchange programmes, such as promoting intercultural citizenship, also need to be addressed in exchange programmes (and not assumed to occur automatically from experiences abroad). To ensure that programmes meet individual and institutional expectations, it is important, therefore, to tailor programmes accordingly, including faculty-led group programmes. Programmes in culturally and linguistically diverse campuses are likely to provide learning that meets these expectations, as evidenced in the case study in Section 4, though building in further formal and informal opportunities for students to connect with one another may help produce greater benefits.

Incorporating ICA, GE, and intercultural citizenship within exchange educational practices can help connect programmes with internationalisation policies around global responsibilities, as well as help to address student motivations to develop global identities and English skills. These areas contrast with practices that focus on native speaker standard norms and educational characterisations of culture based on comparisons at the national level. To incorporate ICA, GE, and intercultural citizenship education, opportunities for diverse intercultural communication experiences should be provided in study and socialisation alongside other international students. While there may be some practical advantages in faculty-led university-organised programmes (in terms of planning and management), programmes may be more effective in terms of HE internationalisation by building in more independent socialisation opportunities as well as opportunities to work alongside other international students (e.g., group projects, social events). If the objective of HE internationalisation is to develop openness to, and skills for engagement with, multicultural communities, then increasing opportunities to connect with a diverse range of partners is more likely to align with these internationalisation aims.

5.3.2 Home University-Based Learning Support

Home universities play an important role in providing support and reflection in the predeparture period, particularly as intercultural learning on student exchanges is not guaranteed, (e.g., Jackson, 2020). In the design of predeparture innovations, practitioners should consider how they may be designed to focus on commonalities, collaboration, and connections with others. Learning may be effective when it is designed around developing awareness of the fluidity of cultures beyond an emphasis on knowledge of specific cultures (i.e., towards ICA level two). Learning can then focus on commonalities among individuals over differences, and it should emphasise connections with communities at different levels (local, national, global). Students should also be provided with explicit content on the concept of intercultural citizenship so that they can design concrete learning goals around developing international identifications (which may also help address vagueness in understandings of 'global' in their motivations). For pre-exchange learning, content on the plurality of Englishes, language ownership, standard language, and examples of ELF/EMF use in multilingual settings may support expanded views towards using English. Indeed, such content may lead to new knowledge as a foundation for developmental multilingual communication experiences during exchanges, in terms of broadening perspectives towards English use. On return, implementing components through independent guided reflections or face-to-face reorientations can help students process their experiences, particularly as students may otherwise remain unaware of what they have learned (Holmes, Bavieri & Ganassin, 2015; Messelink, van Maele, & Spencer-Oatey, 2015). Students may be supported as they identify varied and complex intercultural learning experiences after returning following pedagogically framed guidance designed around ICA, intercultural citizenship, and GE.

5.4 Learning Activities

5.4.1 Introduction

Given this Element's research focus on student exchanges, it is important to incorporate practical aspects that complement the conceptual orientation and help address points raised in the research findings. As such, I now outline a series of learning tasks designed to elicit individual thought on culture and language in communication, to help develop connections with intercultural citizenship, and to help students reflect on the global role of English. These activities may be relevant to pre-departure training or in-exchange learning, or used post-exchange to build on learning. They are organised into five types, each with a specific focus, detailed in each sub-section. On completion of these activities, or activities like them, students should be offered reflective opportunities to consider how individual perspectives may change.

5.4.2 Type One: Reflection and ICA

These activities encourage students to critically examine their own cultural perspectives and assumptions. By engaging in self-reflection, students may become aware of how their perspectives shape their interactions with others. This awareness can be important in exchange settings in terms of navigating diverse intercultural communication experiences.

Cultural Definitions. Provide definitions of culture from an online search, including local examples and essentialist examples. Students consider which definitions they most agree with before they search online for their own definitions. Students then write a summary in an online forum to share their perspectives around the following (adapted from Baker, 2012):

1. What is culture to you?
2. Are definitions important? Why/why not?

The aim is to help students reflect on their own understandings of culture and on any of their own cultural assumptions. By exploring different definitions, students can become aware of complexities in culture, and move beyond essentialist understandings. The online forum promotes discussion and exchange of ideas so students can learn from each other.

Teacher Interviews. Students interview teachers using guiding questions. Questions should stimulate an open exchange of views on any topic of relevance. In these examples, following work on cultures and individuals, students discuss the following with a teacher:

1. What are stereotypes to you?
2. What stereotypes do you know about your teacher's country, your country, your local community?
3. What problems do stereotypes cause?
4. Do you sometimes use stereotypes? If so, when?

This task provides an opportunity for students to discuss different perspectives on stereotypes and culture, including on the impact of stereotypes on different levels of community. The task encourages students to reflect on how to manage stereotypes when engaging with individuals.

Interview Task. Students ask questions to a friend or family member. Encourage students to ask follow-up questions based on responses:

1. What does culture mean to you?
2. How do people in your community show culture?
3. Are there things about your culture you don't like?
4. What can people in your community teach others?
5. What is the impact of others' cultures on you?
6. Have you ever been surprised by the behaviour of someone you've met from another country?
7. What things do you have in common with people from other countries?
8. Have you noticed 'errors' made by a non-native speaker of your first language that did not impede communication?

Students explore their own and others' cultural perspectives through personal connections. Using open-ended and follow-up questions, they should aim to think about commonalities among people. By engaging with friends or family members, students can gain insight into other perspectives.

Roleplays. Students work in groups to define 'common sense' according to individual/local perspectives. They make a list of ten 'common sense' behaviours and then work together to consider alternative common sense, acting these behaviours out via roleplays in classrooms/videos for other students to think about.

By working in groups and defining common sense from different perspectives, students reflect on their own cultural assumptions and how they compare with those of others. By considering alternative behaviours, they can gain an understanding of different perspectives based on different reasoning.

5.4.3 Type Two: Dialogues

Activities that involve dialogue and interactions with other individuals provide opportunities for students to engage directly with different perspectives. These experiences may enhance ICA by allowing students to share experiences, perspectives, and insights.

Find Someone Who. Students complete a 'Find someone who … ' task, completed outside class over a defined period of time (one to two weeks). Students seek respondents with characteristics outlined in items and ask follow-up questions. The aim is to collect different perspectives and reflect. Possible items: [Find someone who …] has travelled overseas; has studied abroad; has a different eye colour to you; wants to live in another city; has had their name spelt incorrectly; reads books by non-local authors; is interested in the same future job as you; is interested in a different future job than you; has a hometown in another country; is interested in a particular country; has different fashion style to you; has used English in the last week; regularly speaks a non-standard language dialect; can speak a language that is not English or Japanese; has a friend in another country; has had a successful intercultural communication experience.

In this task, students seek out individuals with different characteristics and experiences. By asking follow-up questions and collecting different perspectives, they can think about both differences and commonalities among people, including those of a similar background. This task also promotes reflection and self-awareness, as students may realise some of their own assumptions through the process.

Email Exchange. Email exchange, or exchanges via social media, communication apps, or online educational forums, can be effective to connect students with students in other settings and learn about new people and new experiences. Students discuss topics (e.g., global issues) or receive questions from teachers to ask one another.

Email exchange is useful for intercultural citizenship education in student exchange training to encourage connections with others from different backgrounds and engage in discussions on various topics. Students may learn about global issues and develop understandings of, and respect for, different perspectives.

Interviews. Students prepare interview questions for international students in their university communities (if interviewees are willing). It may be possible to arrange particular events at which interviews can be conducted such as international student fairs, language exchange events, intercultural educational workshops, or international student club meetings. Interview questions should be designed to avoid surface-level cultural representations by focusing on commonality and community.

Students engage in conversations with international students in their university community. Through these interviews, students can practise intercultural communication skills, gain understanding of others, and connect with others in the (multicultural) community.

University Events. Organising social events may be designed around sports activities, student parties, video game competitions, movie evenings, and student discussion events.

Through collaboration, students engage in communication and problem-solving while working with students from different backgrounds. The organisation of events, and the events themselves, are opportunities for intercultural learning through engagement with others.

5.4.4 Type Three: Observations

Engaging in observation of real-world situations can help students to examine their surroundings and think about different practices. Students may become more attuned to intercultural differences and similarities and more aware of diversity around them in home or exchange settings.

Looking around You. Students visit a public space (e.g., train station, university cafeteria) and discreetly observe other people. Guiding questions might include: What languages can be heard? How are the students connected to other people? Students write short reports about their observations and are challenged to avoid stereotyping in descriptions.

The task encourages students to be mindful of diversity around them while observing people in a public space. The task may also help students to reflect on their own perspectives and challenge stereotypes.

Analysing Photographs. The following activity is based on *Oxfam Global Citizenship in the Classroom: A Guide for Teachers*, available at https://oxfami library.openrepository.com/. Locate four or five photos online of people involved in current news affairs in different international locations. Include photos without obvious identifying features (e.g., flags, famous people). Students look at the photographs and answer questions:

1. Where do you think the photo is from? Why?
2. What do you think might be happening outside the frame of the photo? Why?

3. What do you think happened before the photo was taken? Why?
4. What do you think happened after the photo was taken? Why?

The task encourages students to critically reflect on different perspectives by putting themselves in the shoes of others. This task helps students to connect with peoples' complex lives in different parts of the world and think about the diversity of perspectives.

English in the Community. Students explore uses of English in their localities and take three photos of English use (e.g., signs, posters, menus, etc.). Photos are posted online forum, with answers to the following:

1. Where was each photo taken?
2. What does each photo show?
3. Why is English included in the examples?
4. What are your thoughts on the use of English in each photo?

By taking photos, students reflect on how English is used in their immediate environment. The task prompts students to analyse the use of English in different contexts and to consider why it is included in certain examples. This aims to help students think critically about the global spread of English.

5.4.5 Type Four: Research for GE Understanding

Research activities help students explore topics, promoting awareness of GE (in particular ELF/EMF). By conducting research, students may gain a broader perspective towards GE and intercultural communication.

Textbook Research. Students select any English textbook and conduct a research task by answering the following (responses shared on an online forum):

1. Which textbook did you select?
2. Why did you select this textbook?
3. Which countries are represented in the textbook?
4. How many native speakers are represented in the textbook?
5. How many non-native speakers?
6. To what extent is there representation of cultural diversity? How do you feel about that?
7. Do you think the textbook is useful for intercultural communication?

By analysing a textbook, students can identify any biases or omissions in the content and become more aware of how different cultures and varieties of English are represented in the materials they use. This task can also help students develop their intercultural communication skills by reflecting on how the textbook may or may not prepare them for interactions with people from different linguistic and cultural backgrounds during student exchange.

YouTube Research. Students find a YouTube video of someone (same first-language user) using English on any topic, and answer the following:

• What do you think about the person's accent?
• Do you think the person uses English successfully?
• What is good about the person's English?
• What connections are there between the person and you?

This task can help students to develop a more inclusive perspective of the English language and to appreciate the diversity of English. Additionally, by reflecting on the connections they have with the person in the videos, students may build confidence in their own ways of using English.

Research Diversity in English Use. Students work in small groups to analyse and compare different ways English is used in specific locations as a means to promote awareness of diversity in English use. Students find audio examples or video clips of people speaking English from particular locations. Research can be shared in presentation tasks, including maps and images. Following presentations, class discussions on understanding and valuing linguistic diversity can help students to reflect on how new awareness of GE (focusing on ELF/EMF) may inform their own language use and communication practices.

The tasks aim to help students see that English is not monolithic, but diverse and constantly evolving.

Students may develop understandings of English as a global language and its impact on the world. For student exchanges in diverse settings, this kind of task may provide important foundational learning for intercultural communication using English with different partners overseas.

5.4.6 Type Five: Intercultural citizenship

These activities aim to connect learning to intercultural citizenship and help build responsibility towards other communities, beyond local and national communities. By engaging in, and reflecting on these activities, students may develop understandings of the interconnectedness of different communities in the world.

Reflecting on the World. In groups, students discuss global news events and make a list of a few in which they are interested. Students engage with these news events and critically reflect on the impact of these events on individuals and communities worldwide. As events may not have a direct impact on the students' lives, teachers can provide questions to encourage connections with other perspectives. Students then consider solutions to problems in their selected events, shared in classwork/online forums.

By discussing and reflecting on these events, students can think about the interconnectedness of global issues and the importance of collaboration and intercultural communication in addressing these issues. Additionally, the task encourages students to consider the perspectives and experiences of other individuals, which can support a connection with intercultural citizenship.

Self-Selected Texts. Students select two news articles (in any language, using internet translations tools) covering the same item and write a summary of the issue. They also consider the following:

1. Why is this issue important to you?
2. Why is this issue important to your local community?
3. Why is this issue important for your country?
4. Why is this issue important to the global community?
5. How did reading about this issue make you feel?
6. What activities can someone engage in to share information about this issue, or help in some way?

By selecting news articles in different languages, students are exposed to diverse perspectives. The prompts encourage students to think about the relevance of the issue from a personal to a global level, and to reflect on their responses and potential actions they can take.

Sustainable Development Goals. Students select and focus on one United Nations Sustainable Development Goal (SDG) and answer the following, based on online research:

1. Why is it important to you?
2. Why is it important to your university community?
3. Why is it important to your country?
4. Why is it important to the global community?
5. What action can you take to support this SDG?
6. How can you work with other individuals to support this SDG?

On completion, students make a poster that can be used in tasks in other classes (e.g., wall readings in which teachers write a list of questions based on the posters, then put up posters on walls around classrooms so that students can read each poster as they seek answers to questions provided by the teacher). Posters can also be displayed elsewhere on campuses.

This task helps students develop their understanding of particular issues and how they connect to their local communities and the global community. By focusing on SDGs, students can consider how different communities react to global issues.

Newspaper-Making: Students receive a set of photos (twenty to thirty), presented on paper or online, of current global events. Students work in groups and select two photos of particular individual concern. They design a newspaper front cover with written reports and headlines alongside their photos. On completion, work can be shared with others for discussion.

Here, students engage with current global events by selecting and analysing photos. Students think critically about different perspectives and consider the impact of these events on individuals in different communities. Working in groups also promotes collaboration, and sharing different work can lead to further insights about the issues presented.

As stated in Section 5.4.1, it is crucial to provide opportunities for students to reflect following engagement in these tasks (which may be used in pre-departure training, in-exchange learning, and in post-sojourn learning). By combining the concepts in this research with practical learning, and addressing issues raised in the findings, exchange students may have more impactful learning experiences.

5.5 Conclusion

The learning activities outlined aim to combine practical learning with the conceptual position in this Element. I have argued that learning on short-term student exchanges that focuses on target-culture learning and target standard English language practices overlooks the multicultural and multilingual aspects of many sojourns and the important contribution this diversity can make to individual learning. I have also attempted to challenge assumptions that student exchanges lead solely to knowledge and experience of local cultures and languages, and interactions with local individuals. Moreover, I have criticised views that contact with native language users is responsible for more effective learning outcomes. In doing so, I have emphasised the multicultural character of many exchanges where students encounter other individuals whose cultural frames of reference and individual identities go beyond what may be learnt or predicted in fact-based cultural learning. I have also argued that English use on student exchanges is more fluid than in its common educational representations and that experiences of intercultural communication during student exchanges can lead to new perspectives towards English use, linked to GE, and in particular, to ELF/EMF.

These findings highlight the importance of a flexible and context-specific approach to intercultural communication on student exchanges, which should be reflected in research and educational practices. I advocate for ICA as an important framework for understanding complex intercultural learning in culturally and linguistically diverse exchange contexts, and understandings of how students navigate this complexity in communication with individuals from other backgrounds. I also contend that intercultural citizenship education is important for exchange students given HE aims to prepare individuals to communicate and interact effectively in a diverse and interconnected world by developing skills to understand and engage with individuals in multicultural contexts. I have argued that the role of student exchanges can be valuable to a connection with intercultural citizenship and that this is highly relevant to HE internationalisation.

Intercultural awareness and intercultural citizenship education may be used to inform educational design on both student exchanges and home university-based pre-departure and post-exchange learning innovations. The integration of GE themes and practices in such learning aims to promote pluralistic understandings of English, recognition and acceptance of variability in English language use, and acceptance of, and willingness to use, ELF/EMF in communication. In this combined educational approach, students may be better prepared for the opportunities and challenges in an interconnected world, and thus, HE statements around internationalisation may be more effectively supported following these short-term student exchange experiences that are widely promoted by universities.

References

Abdzadeh, Y., & Baker, W. (2020). Cultural awareness in an Iranian English language classroom: A teaching intervention in an interculturally 'conservative' setting. *Journal of English as a Lingua Franca, 9*(1), 57–80. https://doi.org/10.1515/jelf-2020-2030.

Alismail, H. A. (2016). Multicultural education: Teachers' perceptions and preparation. *Journal of Education and Practice, 7*(11), 139–46.

Allen, H. W. (2010). Interactive contact as linguistic affordance during short-term study abroad: Myth or reality? *Frontiers: The Interdisciplinary Journal of Study Abroad, 19*, 1–26. https://doi.org/10.36366/frontiers.v19i1.271.

Anderson, P. H., Lawton, L., Rexeisen, R. J., & Hubbard, A. C. (2006). Short-term study abroad and intercultural sensitivity: A pilot study. *International Journal of Intercultural Relations, 30*, 457–69. https://doi.org/10.1016/j.ijintrel.2005.10.004.

Babaii, E. (2018). Multiculturalism: An asset or a problem? Implications for intercultural education. *Intercultural Communication Education, 1*(2), 45–53. https://dx.doi.org/10.29140/ice.v1n2.65.

Bachman, L. F. (1990). *Fundamental Considerations in Language Testing.* Oxford: Oxford University Press.

Baker, W. (2011). Intercultural awareness: Modelling an understanding of cultures in intercultural communication through English as a lingua franca. *Language and Intercultural Communication, 11*(3), 197–214. https://doi.org/10.1080/14708477.2011.577779.

Baker, W. (2012). *Using E-Learning to Develop Intercultural Awareness in ELT: A Critical Education in a Thai Higher Education Setting.* London: British Council.

Baker, W. (2015). *Culture and Identity Through English as a Lingua Franca: Rethinking Concepts and Goals in Intercultural Communication.* Berlin: De Gruyter.

Baker, W., & Ishikawa, T. (2021). *Transcultural Communication through Global Englishes: An Advanced Textbook for Students.* London: Routledge.

Baker, W., Boonsuk, Y., Ra, J. J., Sangiamchit, C., & Snodin, N. (2022). Thai study abroad students as intercultural citizens: Developing intercultural citizenship through English medium education and ELT, *Asia Pacific Journal of Education.* Advance online publication. https://doi.org/10.1080/02188791.2022.2096569.

Baker-Smemoe, W., Dewey, D. P., Bown, J., & Martinsen, R. A. (2014). Variables affecting L2 gains during study abroad. *Foreign Language Annals, 47*(3), 464–86. https://doi.org/10.1111/flan.12093.

Barrett, M., & Golubeva, I. (2022). From intercultural communicative competence to intercultural citizenship: Preparing young people for citizenship in a culturally diverse democratic world. In T. McConachy, I. Golubeva, & M. Wagner (Eds.), *Intercultural Learning in Language Education and Beyond* (pp. 60–83). Bristol: Multilingual Matters.

Beelen, J., & Jones, E. (2015). Redefining internationalization at home. In A. Curaj, L. Matei, R. Pricopie, J. Salmi, & P. Scott (Eds.), *The European Higher Education Area: Between Critical Reflections and Future Policies* (pp. 59–72). London: Springer.

Brotherhood, T., Hammond, C. D., & Kim, Y. (2019). Towards an actor-centered typology of internationalization: A study of junior international faculty in Japanese universities. *Higher Education, 79*, 497–514. https://doi.org/10.1007/s10734-019-00420-5.

Brown, C. A. (2019). Foreign faculty tokenism, English, and 'internationalization' in a Japanese university. *Asia Pacific Journal of Education, 39*(3), 404–16. https://doi.org/10.1080/02188791.2019.1598850.

Byram, M. (2008). *From Foreign Language Education to Education for Intercultural Citizenship: Essays and Reflections*. Bristol: Multilingual Matters.

Byram, M., Golubeva, I., Han, H., & Wagner, M. (Eds.) (2017). *From Principles to Practice in Education for Intercultural Citizenship*. Bristol: Multilingual Matters.

Byrne, B. (2004). Qualitative interviewing. In C. Seale (Ed.), *Researching Society and Culture* (2nd ed., pp. 179–92). London: SAGE Publications.

Canale, M. (1983). From communicative competence to communicative language pedagogy. In J. C. Richards & R. W. Schmidt (Eds.), *Language and Communication* (pp. 2–27). London: Longman.

Canale, M., & Swain, M. (1980). Theoretical bases of communicative approaches to second language teaching and testing. *Applied Linguistics, 1*(1), 1–47. https://doi.org/10.1093/applin/I.1.1.

Carroll, J. B. (1967). Foreign language proficiency levels attained by language majors near graduation from college. *Foreign Language Annals, 1*(2), 131–51. https://doi.org/10.1111/j.1944-9720.1967.tb00127.x.

Chieffo, L., & Griffiths, L. (2004). Large-scale assessment of student attitudes after a short-term study abroad program. *Frontiers: The Interdisciplinary Journal of Study Abroad, 10*(1), 165–77. https://doi.org/10.36366/frontiers.v10i1.140.

Çiftçi, E. Y., & Karaman, A. C. (2018). 'I do not have to love them, I'm just interested in their language': Preparation for a study abroad period and the negotiation(s) of intercultural competence. *Language and Intercultural Communication, 18*(6), 595–612. https://doi.org/10.1080/14708477.2017.1374391.

Coleman, J. A. (2013). Researching whole people and whole lives. In C. Kinginger (Ed.), *Social and Cultural Aspects of Language Learning in Study Abroad* (pp. 17–44). Amsterdam: John Benjamins.

Crystal, D. (2008). Two thousand million? *English Today, 24*(1), 3–6. https://doi.org/10.1017/S0266078408000023.

Csizér, K., & Kontra, E. H. (2012). ELF, ESP, ENL and their effect on students' aims and beliefs: A structural equation model. *System, 40*, 1–10. https://doi.org/10.1016/j.system.2012.01.002.

Cubillos, J., & Ilvento, T. (2018). Intercultural contact in short-term study abroad programs. *Hispania, 101*(2), 249–66. http://dx.doi.org/10.1353/hpn.2018.0117.

Day, J. T. (1987). Student motivation, academic validity, and the summer language program abroad: An editorial. *Modern Language Journal, 71*(3), 261–6. https://doi.org/10.1111/j.1540-4781.1987.tb00365.x.

De Wit, H. (2020). The future of internationalization of higher education in challenging global contexts. *ETD Educação Temática Digital, 22*(3), 538–45. https://doi.org/10.20396/etd.v22i3.8659471.

Dewey, M. (2007). English as a lingua franca and globalisation: an interconnected perspective. *International Journal of Applied Linguistics, 17*(3), 332–53. https://doi.org/10.1111/j.1473-4192.2007.00177.x.

Dippold, D., Bridges, S., Eccles, S., & Mullen, E. (2019). Developing the global graduate: How first year university students narrate their experiences of culture. *Language and Intercultural Communication, 19*(4), 313–27. https://doi.org/10.1080/14708477.2018.1526939.

Donnelly-Smith, L. (2009). Global learning through short-term study abroad. *Association of American Colleges and Universities Peer Review, 11*(Fall), 12–15. Accessed December 17, 2022, from http://catcher.sandiego.edu/items/cee/Reading4.Short-term%20SA.pdf.

Dorsett, P., Larmar, S., & Clark, J. (2019). Transformative intercultural learning: A short-term international study tour. *Journal of Social Work Education, 55*(3), 565–78. https://doi.org/10.1080/10437797.2018.1548984.

Eades, J., Goodman, R., & Hada, Y. (Eds.). (2005). *The 'Big Bang' in Japanese Higher Education: The 2004 Reforms and the Dynamics of Change.* Melbourne: Trans-Pacific Press.

Engle, L., & Engle, J. (2003). Study abroad levels: Toward a classification of program types. *Frontiers: The Interdisciplinary Journal of Study Abroad, 9* (1), 1–20. https://doi.org/10.36366/frontiers.v9i1.113.

Fang, F., & Baker, W. (2018). 'A more inclusive mind towards the world': English language teaching and study abroad in China from intercultural citizenship and English as a lingua franca perspectives. *Language Teaching Research, 22*(5), 608–24. https://doi.org/10.1177/1362168817718574.

Fang, F., & Baker, W. (2021). Implementing a critical pedagogy of Global Englishes in ELT from the lens of EMI and intercultural citizenship. In Y. Bayyurt & M. Saraceni (Eds.), *Bloomsbury World Englishes Volume 3: Pedagogies* (pp. 177–91). London: Bloomsbury.

Fantini, A. E. (2012). Multiple strategies for assessing intercultural communicative competence. In J. Jackson (Ed.), *The Routledge Handbook of Language and Intercultural Communication* (pp. 390–405). London: Routledge.

Ferguson, G. (2007). The global spread of English, scientific communication and ESP: Questions of equity, access, and domain loss. *Ibérica, 13*, 7–38.

Forum on Education Abroad (2011). *Education Abroad Glossary* (2nd ed.). Carlisle, PA: Forum on Education Abroad.

Gaia, A. C. (2015). Short-term faculty-led study abroad programs enhance cultural exchange and self-awareness. *The International Education Journal: Comparative Perspectives, 14*(1), 21–31.

Golubeva, I., Wagner, M., & Yakimowski, M. E. (2017). Comparing students' perceptions of global citizenship in Hungary and the USA. In M. Byram, I. Golubeva, H. Han, & M. Wagner (Eds.), *From Principles to Practice in Education for Intercultural Citizenship* (pp. 3–24). Bristol: Multilingual Matters.

Gorski, P. C. (2008). Good intentions are not enough: A decolonizing intercultural education. *Intercultural Education, 19*(6), 515–25. https://doi.org/ 10.1080/14675980802568319.

Gottlieb, N. (2008). Japan: Language policy and planning in transition. *Current Issues in Language Planning, 9*(1), 1–68. https://doi.org/10.2167/cilp116.0.

Gundara, J. S., & Portera, A. (2008). Theoretical reflections on intercultural education. *Intercultural Education, 19*(6), 463–8. https://doi.org/10.1080/ 14675980802568244.

Han, H., Li, S., Hongtao, J., & Yuqin, Z. (2017). Exploring perceptions of intercultural citizenship among English learners in Chinese universities. In M. Byram, I. Golubeva, H. Han, & M. Wagner (Eds.), *From Principles to Practice in Education for Intercultural Citizenship* (pp. 25–44). Bristol: Multilingual Matters.

Heinzmann, S., Künzle, R., Schallhart, N., & Müller, M. (2015). The effect of study abroad on intercultural competence: Results from a longitudinal quasi-experimental study. *Frontiers: The Interdisciplinary Journal of Study Abroad, 26*(1), 187–208. https://doi.org/10.36366/frontiers.v26i1.366.

Holliday, A., Hyde, M., & Kullman, J. (2021). *Intercultural Communication: An Advanced Resource Book for Students* (4th ed.). London: Routledge.

Holmes, P., Bavieri, L., & Ganassin, S. (2015). Developing intercultural understanding for study abroad: Students' and teachers' perspectives on pre-departure intercultural learning. *Intercultural Education, 26*(1), 16–30. https://doi.org/10.1080/14675986.2015.993250.

Huang, F. (2009). The internationalization of the academic profession in Japan: A quantitative perspective. *Journal of Studies in International Education, 13*(2), 143–58. https://doi.org/10.1177/1028315308331101.

Hughes, P. C., & Baldwin, J. R. (2002). Communication and stereotypical impressions. *The Howard Journal of Communication, 13*, 113–28. https://doi.org/10.1080/10646170290089917.

Humphreys, G. (2022). Short-term study abroad: Developing Global Englishes awareness. *Englishes in Practice, 5*(1), 133–60. https://doi.org/10.2478/eip-2022-0006.

Humphreys, G., & Baker, W. (2021). Developing intercultural awareness from short-term study abroad: Insights from an interview study of Japanese students. *Language and Intercultural Communication, 21*(2), 260–75. https://doi.org/10.1080/14708477.2020.1860997.

Humphries, S., & Burns, A. (2015). 'In reality it's almost impossible': CLT-oriented curriculum change. *ELT Journal, 69*(3), 239–48. https://doi.org/10.1093/elt/ccu081.

Hynninen, N., & Solin, A. (2017). Language norms in ELF. In J. Jenkins, M. Dewey, & W. Baker (Eds.), *The Routledge Handbook of English as a Lingua Franca* (pp. 267–78). Abingdon: Routledge.

IEREST (2015). *Intercultural Education Resources for Erasmus Students and Their Teachers*. Koper: Annales University Press. www.ierest-project.eu/.

Isabelli-García, C. (2006). Study abroad social networks, motivation and attitudes: Implications for second language acquisition. In E. Churchill & M. DuFon (Eds.), *Language Learners in Study Abroad Contexts* (pp. 231–58). Clevedon: Multilingual Matters.

Ishikawa, T. (2021). Global Englishes and 'Japanese English'. *Asian Englishes, 23*(1), 15–29. https://doi.org/10.1080/13488678.2020.1858579.

Jackson, J. (2020). The language and intercultural dimension of education abroad. In J. Jackson (Ed.), *The Routledge Handbook of Language and Intercultural Communication* (2nd ed., pp. 442–56). London: Routledge.

Japan Association of Overseas Studies (JAOS) (2021). *JAOS Survey Report 2021 and JAOS Guidelines*. www.jaos.or.jp/news-eng/jaos-survey-report-2021-and-jaos-guidelines-2.

JASSO (2022). *JASSO outline 2022–2023*. www.jasso.go.jp/en/about/organiza tion/icsFiles/afieldfile/2022/09/08/e2022-2023_outline all.pdf.

JASSO (2018). *Nendo nihonjin gakusei ryūgaku jokyou chousa kekka [Results of the survey on Japanese students studying abroad]*. www.studyinjapan.go.jp/ja/ statistics/nippon/data/2018.html.

Jenkins, J. (2015a). Repositioning English and multilingualism in English as a lingua Franca. *Englishes in Practice*, *2*(3), 49–85. https://doi.org/10.1515/ eip-2015-0003.

Jenkins, J. (2015b). *Global Englishes: A Resource Book for Students* (3rd ed.). Abingdon: Routledge.

Jenkins, J., Cogo, A., & Dewey, M. (2011). Review of developments in research into English as a lingua franca. *Language Teaching*, *44*(3), 281–315. https:// doi.org/10.1017/S0261444811000115.

Jones, E. (2017). Problematising and reimagining the notion of 'international student experience', *Studies in Higher Education*, *42*(5), 933–43. https://doi .org/10.1080/03075079.2017.1293880.

Kachru, B. B. (1982). *The Other Tongue: English Across Cultures*. Chicago: University of Illinois Press.

Kachru, B. B., Kachru, Y., & Nelson, C. L. (2006). *The Handbook of World Englishes*. Oxford: Blackwell.

Karakaş, A. (2021). Avowed objectives in ELT curriculum versus ground realities in classrooms: How convergent are they? In K. Büyükkarcı & A. Önal (Eds.), *Essentials of Applied Linguistics and Foreign Language Teaching: 21st Century Skills and Classroom Applications* (pp. 102–20). Istanbul: ISRES Publishing.

Kehl, K., & Morris, J. (2008). Differences in global-mindedness between short-term and semester-long study abroad participants at selected private universities. *Frontiers: The Interdisciplinary Journal of Study Abroad*, *15*(1), 67–79. https://doi.org/10.36366/frontiers.v15i1.217.

Kelo, M., Teichler, U., & Wächter, B. (Eds.). (2006). *Eurodata: Student Mobility in European Higher Education*. Bonn: Lemmens.

Kikuchi, K., & Sakai, H. (2009). Japanese learners' demotivation to study English: A survey study. *JALT Journal*, *31*(2), 183–204.

Killick, D. (2015). *Developing the Global Student: Higher Education in an Era of Globalization*. London: Routledge.

Kinginger, C. (2009). *Language Learning and Study Abroad: A Critical Reading of the Research*. New York: Palgrave MacMillan.

Knight, J. (2008). *Higher Education in Turmoil: The Changing World of Internationalisation*. Rotterdam: Sense Publishers.

Koyanagi, S. (2018). Impact of intercultural communication during short-term study-abroad of Japanese students: Analysis from a perspective of cognitive modification. *Journal of Intercultural Communication Research, 47*(2), 105–20. https://doi.org/10.1080/17475759.2018.1435423.

Kubota, R. (2016). The social imaginary of study abroad: complexities and contradictions. *The Language Learning Journal, 44*(3), 347–57. https://doi.org/10.1080/09571736.2016.1198098

Kuntz, P., & Belnap, R. K. (2001). Beliefs about language learning held by teachers and their students at two Arabic programs abroad. *Al-'Arabiyya, 34*, 91–113.

Kurt, M. R., Olitsky, N. H., & Geis, P. (2013). Assessing global awareness over short-term study abroad sequence: A factor analysis. *Frontiers: The Interdisciplinary Journal of Study Abroad, 23*(1), 22–41. https://doi.org/10.36366/frontiers.v23i1.327.

Kusumaningputri, R., & Widodo, H. P. (2018). Promoting Indonesian university students' critical intercultural awareness in tertiary EAL classrooms: The use of digital photograph-mediated intercultural tasks. *System, 72*, 49–61. https://doi.org/10.1016/j.system.2017.10.003.

Li, W. (2018). Translanguaging as a practical theory of language. *Applied Linguistics, 39*(1), 9–30. https://doi.org/10.1093/applin/amx039.

Llanes, A., Arnó, E., & Mancho-Barés, G. (2016). Erasmus students using English as a lingua franca: Does study abroad in a non-English-speaking country improve L2 English? *The Language Learning Journal, 44*(3), 292–303. https://doi.org/10.1080/09571736.2016.1198099.

Lörz, M., Netz, N., & Quast, H. (2016). Why do students from underprivileged families less often intend to study abroad? *Higher Education, 72*, 153–74. https://doi.org/10.1007/s10734-015-9943-1.

Matsuda, A. (2017). *Introduction*. In A. Matsuda (Ed.), *Preparing Teachers to Teach English as an International Language* (pp. xiii–xxii). Bristol: Multilingual Matters.

Mayumi, K., & Hüttner, J. (2020). Changing beliefs on English: Study abroad for teacher development. *ELT Journal, 74*(3), 268–76. https://doi.org/10.1093/elt/ccaa020.

McConachy, T. (2018). Critically engaging with cultural representations in foreign language textbooks. *Intercultural Education, 29*(1), 77–88. https://doi.org/10.1080/14675986.2017.1404783.

McCrostie, J. (2017, Aug 2017). More Japanese may be studying abroad, but not for long. *Japan Times.* www.japantimes.co.jp/community/2017/08/09/ issues/japanese-may-studying-abroad-not-long/#.XKfampgzbIU.

McKay, S. (2018). English as an international language: What it is and what it means for pedagogy. *RELC Journal, 49*(1), 9–23. https://doi.org/10.1177/ 0033688217738817.

Messelink, H. E., Van Maele, J., & Spencer-Oatey, H. (2015). Intercultural competencies: What students in study and placement mobility should be learning. *Intercultural Education, 26*(1), 62–72. https://doi.org/10.1080/ 14675986.2015.993555.

MEXT (2017). *Shōgakkō gakusyū shidou youryou kaisetsu – Gaikokugo hen [Elementary school curriculum and instruction guide: Foreign language].* Tokyo: Toyokan. www.econfn.com/ssk/kougi/syougakusidou.pdf.

Mihut, G., de Gayardon, A., & Rudt, Y. (2017). The long-term mobility of international faculty: A literature review. In M. Yudkevich, P. G. Altbach, & L. E. Rumbley (Eds.), *International Faculty in Higher Education: Comparative Perspectives on Recruitment, Integration, and Impact* (pp. 13–31). London: Routledge.

Miles, M. B., Huberman, A. M., & Saldaña, J. (2014). *Qualitative Data Analysis: A Methods Sourcebook* (3rd ed.). London: SAGE Publications.

Mitchell, R., McManus, K., & Tracy-Ventura, N. (2015). Placement type and language learning during residence abroad. In R. Mitchell, N. Tracy-Ventura, & K. McManus (Eds.), *Social Interaction, Identity and Language Learning During Residence Abroad* (pp. 115–37). Amsterdam: European Second Language Association.

Mocanu, V., & Llurda, E. (2020). Constructing and reconstructing attitudes towards language learning in study abroad. In A. Bocanegra-Valle (Ed.), *Applied Linguistics and Knowledge Transfer: Internationalisation, Employability and Social Challenges* (pp. 181–202). Berlin: Peter Lang.

Mondi, M., Woods, P., & Rafi, A. (2007). Students' 'uses and gratification expectancy' conceptual framework in relation to e-learning resources. *Asia Pacific Education Review, 8*(3), 435–49. https://doi.org/10.1007/BF03026472.

Oda, M. (2018). A post-EFL approach to the administration of English language programs. *JACET ELF SIG Journal, 2*, 30–38.

Ota, H. (2018). Internationalization of higher education: Global trends and Japan's challenges. *Educational Studies in Japan: International Yearbook, 12*, 91–105. https://doi.org/10.7571/esjkyoiku.12.91.

Perry, L., Stoner, L. & Tarrant, M. (2012). More than a vacation: Short-term study abroad as a critically reflective, transformative learning experience. *Creative Education, 3*(5), 679–83. https://doi.org/10.4236/ce.2012.35101.

Piller, I. (2017). *Intercultural Communication: A Critical Introduction.* Edinburgh: Edinburgh University Press.

Pipitone, J. M. (2018). Place as pedagogy: Toward study abroad for social change. *Journal of Experiential Education, 41*(1), 54–74. https://doi.org/ 10.1177/1053825917751509.

Poole, G. S. (2016). Administrative practices as institutional identity: Bureaucratic impediments to HE 'internationalisation' policy in Japan. *Comparative Education, 52*(1), 62–77. https://doi.org/10.1080/03050068 .2015.1125615.

Porto, M. (2014). Intercultural citizenship education in an EFL online project in Argentina. *Language and Intercultural Communication, 14*(2), 245–61. https://doi.org/10.1080/14708477.2014.890625.

Risager, K. (2022). Intercultural communicative competence: transnational and decolonial developments. In T. McConachy, I. Golubeva, & M. Wagner (Eds.), *Intercultural Learning in Language Education and Beyond* (pp. 3–21). Bristol: Multilingual Matters.

Rodrik, D. (2011). *The Globalization Paradox.* Oxford: Oxford University Press.

Rose, H., & Galloway, N. (2019). *Global Englishes for Language Teaching.* Cambridge: Cambridge University Press.

Rose, R., Sahan, K., & Zhou, S. (2022). Global English medium instruction: Perspectives at the crossroads of global Englishes and EMI. *Asian Englishes, 24*(2), 160–172. https://doi.org/10.1080/13488678.2022.2056794.

Sakui, K. (2004). Wearing two pairs of shoes: Language teaching in Japan. *ELT Journal, 58*(2), 155–63. https://doi.org/10.1093/elt/58.2.155.

Salih, A. A., & Omar, L. I. (2021). Globalized English and users' intercultural awareness: Implications for internationalization of higher education. *Citizenship, Social and Economics Education, 20*(3), 181–96. https://doi .org/10.1177/20471734211037660.

Schartner, A. (2016). The effect of study abroad on intercultural competence: A longitudinal case study of international postgraduate students at a British university. *Journal of Multilingual and Multicultural Development, 37*(4), 402–18. https://doi.org/10.1080/01434632.2015.1073737.

Scollon, R., Scollon, S. W., & Jones, R. H. (2012). *Intercultural Communication: A Discourse Approach* (3rd ed.). Oxford: Blackwell.

Seidlhofer, B. (2003). *A Concept of International English and Related Issues: From 'Real English' to 'Realist English'?* Language Policy Division: Council of Europe. https://rm.coe.int/a-concept-of-international-english-and-related-issues-from-real-englis/168088782f.

Seidlhofer, B. (2011). *Understanding English as a Lingua Franca*. Oxford: Oxford University Press.

Selvi, A. F. (2010). All teachers are equal, but some teachers are more equal than others: Trend analysis of job advertisements in English language teaching. *WATESOL NNEST Caucus Annual Review, 1*(1), 155–81.

Sharifian, F. (2013). Globalisation and developing metacultural competence in learning English as an international language. *Multilingual Education, 3*(1), 1–11. https://doi.org/10.1186/2191-5059-3-7.

Shiveley, J., & Misco, T. (2015). Long-term impacts of short-term study abroad: teacher perceptions of preservice study abroad experiences. *Frontiers: The Interdisciplinary Journal of Study Abroad, 26*(1), 107–20. https://doi.org/10.36366/frontiers.v26i1.361.

Sifakis, N. C. (2019). ELF awareness in English language teaching: Principles and processes. *Applied Linguistics, 40*(2), 288–306. https://doi.org/10.1080/13488678.2018.1544700.

Silverman, D. (2014). *Interpreting Qualitative Data* (5th ed.). London: SAGE Publications.

Slotkin, M. H., Durie, C. J. and Eisenberg, J. R. (2012). The benefits of short-term study abroad as blended learning experience. *Journal of International Education in Business, 4*(2), 163–73. https://doi.org/10.1108/18363261211281762.

Soria, K. M., & Troisi, J. (2014). Internationalization at home alternatives to study abroad: Implications for students' development of global, international, and intercultural competencies. *Journal of Studies in International Education, 18*(3), 261–80. https://doi.org/10.1177/1028315313496572.

Stewart, A., & Miyahara, M. (2011). Parallel universes: Globalization and identity in English language teaching at a Japanese university. In P. Seargeant (Ed.), *English in Japan in the Era of Globalization* (pp. 60–79). New York: Palgrave Macmillan.

Stewart, T. (2009). Will the new English curriculum for 2013 work? *The Language Teacher, 33*(11), 9–13.

Sugimoto, Y. (2003). *An Introduction to Japanese Society*. Cambridge: Cambridge University Press.

Sugimura, M. (2015). The mobility of international students and higher education policies in Japan. *The Gakushuin Journal of International Studies, 2*, 1–19. https://core.ac.uk/download/pdf/292915046.pdf.

Tanaka, F. (2010). A survey-based study of Japanese university student attitudes toward EIL and implications for the future of English education in Japan. *Asian Englishes, 13*(1), 48–71. https://doi.org/10.1080/13488678.2010.10801272.

Trede, F., Bowles, W., & Bridges, D. (2013). Developing intercultural competence and global citizenship through international experiences: Academics' perceptions. *Intercultural Education*, 24(5), 442–55. https://doi.org/10.1080/14675986.2013.825578.

Trentman, E., & Diao, W. (2021). Introduction: Multilingual approaches to language learning in study abroad. In W. Diao & E. Trentman (Eds.), *Language Learning in Study Abroad: The Multilingual Turn* (pp. 1–12). Bristol: Multilingual Matters.

University of Southampton (2023). *Centre for Global Englishes.* www.southampton.ac.uk/cge/index.page.

Vickers, E. (2018). Internationalising Japanese education: contradictions, challenges and opportunities. *Educational Studies in Japan*, *12*, 1–7. https://doi.org/10.7571/esjkyoiku.12.1.

Wagner, M., & Byram, M. (2018). Intercultural citizenship. In Y. Y. Kim (Ed.), *The International Encyclopedia of Intercultural Communication.* Oxford: Wiley-Blackwell.

Whitsed, C., & Volet, S. (2011). Fostering the intercultural dimensions of internationalisation in higher education: Metaphors and challenges in the Japanese context. *Journal of Studies in International Education*, *15*(2), 146–70. https://doi.org/10.1177/1028315309357941.

Whitsed, C., & Wright, P. (2011). Perspectives from within: Adjunct, foreign, English language teachers in the internationalization of Japanese universities. *Journal of Research in International Education*, *10*(1), 28–45. https://doi.org/10.1177/1475240910396332.

Yamagami, M., & Tollefson, J. W. (2011). Elite discourses of globalization in Japan: The role of English. In P. Seargeant (Ed.), *English in Japan in the Era of Globalization* (pp. 15–37). Basingstoke: Palgrave Macmillan.

Yazan, B. & Rudolph, N. (Eds.) (2018). *Criticality, Teacher Identity, and (In)equity in English Language Teaching: Issues and Implications.* Dordrecht: Springer.

Yonezawa, A., Akiba, H., & Hirouchi, D. (2009). Japanese university leaders' perceptions of internationalization: The role of government in review and support. *Journal of Studies in International Education*, *13*(2), 125–42. https://doi.org/10.1177/1028315308330847.

Yonezawa, Y. (2017). Internationalization management in Japanese universities: the effects of institutional structures and cultures. *Journal of Studies in International Education*, *21*(4), 375–390. https://doi.org/10.1177%2F1028315317706412.

Yu, Q., & van Maele, J. (2018). Fostering intercultural awareness in a Chinese English reading class. *Chinese Journal of Applied Linguistics*, *41*, 357–375. https://doi.org/10.1515/cjal-2018-0027.

Zhu, H. (2019). *Exploring Intercultural Communication: Language in Action* (2nd ed.). London: Routledge.

Zotzmann, K. (2015). The impossibility of defining and measuring intercultural competencies. In D. Rivers (Ed.), *Resistance to 'the Known': Counter-Conduct in Language Education* (pp. 168–91). Basingstoke: Palgrave.

Acknowledgements

I would firstly like to acknowledge the 15 students for their contribution to this project. Secondly, I would like to sincerely thank the series editors, Will Baker, Troy McConachy, and Sonia Morán Panero for their valuable support in preparing this Element. Their guidance has been greatly appreciated throughout the process (and long before). I would also like to thank the anonymous reviewers for their insightful comments and constructive feedback which have contributed significantly to the development of this work. Special thanks to Mika and Saki for their patience and understanding during this endeavour. I dedicate this to Patricia and Alun.

Will Baker
University of Southampton

Will Baker is Director of the Centre for Global Englishes and an Associate Professor of Applied Linguistics, University of Southampton. His research interests are Intercultural and Transcultural Communication, English as a Lingua Franca, English medium education, Intercultural education and ELT, and he has published and presented internationally in all these areas. Recent publications include: *Intercultural and Transcultural Awareness in Language Teaching* (2022), co-author of *Transcultural Communication through Global Englishes* (2021), co-editor of *The Routledge Handbook of English as a Lingua Franca* (2018). He is also co-editor of the book series 'Developments in English as Lingua Franca'.

Troy McConachy
University of Warwick

Troy McConachy is Associate Professor in Applied Linguistics at the University of Warwick. His work aims to make interdisciplinary connections between the fields of language education, intercultural communication, and social psychology, focusing particularly on the role of metapragmatic awareness in intercultural communication and intercultural learning. He is author of *Developing Intercultural Perspectives on Language Use: Exploring Pragmatics and Culture in Foreign Language Learning* (2018), Editor-in-Chief of the international journal *Intercultural Communication Education*, and co-editor of *Teaching and Learning Second Language Pragmatics for Intercultural Understanding* and *Intercultural Learning and Language Education and Beyond: Evolving Concepts, Perspectives and Practices.*

Sonia Morán Panero
University of Southampton

Sonia Morán Panero is a Lecturer in Applied Linguistics at the University of Southampton. Her academic expertise is on the sociolinguistics of the use and learning of English for transcultural communication purposes. Her work has focused particularly on language ideologies around Spanish and English as global languages, English language policies and education in Spanish-speaking settings and English medium instruction on global education. She has published on these areas through international knowledge dissemination platforms such as ELTJ, JELF, *The Routledge Handbook of English as a Lingua Franca* (2018) and the British Council.

About the Series
This series offers a mixture of key texts and innovative research publications from established and emerging scholars which represent the depth and diversity of current intercultural communication research and suggest new directions for the field.

Cambridge Elements $\equiv$

Intercultural Communication

Elements in the Series

.

Printed in the United States
by Baker & Taylor Publisher Services